The Best of

MAKING THINGS

A Hand Book of Creative Discovery

Ann Sayre Wiseman

HAND PRINT PRESS
Oregon

"what we learn to do, we learn by doing" — Aristotle

Hand Print Press: POB 576, Blodgett, OR, 97326, www.handprintpress.com.
Revised, updated, compact edition. This book includes material previously published as *Making Things*, books 1 and 2.

Library of Congress Cataloging-in-Publication Data
Wiseman, Ann Sayre.
The Best of Making Things: A Handbook of Creative Discovery
159 p.: ill; indexed, 6x9 ins.
ISBN 10: 0-9679846-1-0 ISBN 13: 978-0-9679846-1-2
1. Handicraft, 2. Art, 3. Education
TT157.W5923 2005 745.5 dc20

This edition is for Luca & Isaac, from one generation to another, with love

Praise for Previous Editions:

"*Making Things* is great....Surprise, surprise the turtle race will be on ZOOM...it was sent in by one of our viewers...!"

– Christopher Sarson, Executive Producer, **ZOOM,** ***WGBH TV Boston***

"Ann Sayre Wiseman has made a book that is untied to any single task. A teacher of teachers, she has developed the material over 25 years of working among schoolchildren and adults of many ages. For more than 100 activities, the drawings and clear, hand-lettered text take a reader into her cheerful presence. A list will suggest what is here: papermaking in variety; papery products such as simple masks, beads and mobiles; printing from fingertips, from whole scaly fish, from carved potatoes and many variants. The most athletic demand is a nifty page on stilts and stilt walking. The most mathematical is weaving, even at its simplest. The most technological is how to buy electrical conduit or copper tubing, to cut with hacksaw or pipe cutter for music from your new metallophone. Most delicious is the bread sculpture. The author has extended it to produce bread mermaids, crocodiles, and a lion peaceably enfolding a lamb. In sum, the best learning is doing; feedback from failure is often the path to success; take time and path to suit yourself—but the act of creation is often messy! Success is not won simply by whim. Wiseman's book is aimed at guiding the work of hours or days"

– Scientific **American**

"A must for any person at any age who loves to make things, I bought this book because I heard from so many people that it has inspired wonderful ideas. It has provided me with 125 useful and creative projects - I've made them all! Don't miss it! It's for any age, young or old who love to make things!

– Jody Gardner, Amazon.com review

"I haven't even finished reading your book...but...such a creative and simple book on art and all it includes... will undoubtedly be used for my classes...in the North country of Ontario...[and] with adults for Confederation College in Thunder Bay. What else is there to say? I only want you to know I am one of (hopefully many) peoples using your book and its damn honest attitude."

– A. Bandenieks, Thunder Bay Ontario

"...your marvelous book...is so well detailed...If I were to give [it] to someone now, who could practice a lot of the ideas, and start collecting materials, I could be assured of a good and successful summertime-fun workshop. This is exactly what I intend to do. ...Thanks again for your fine and badly needed book."

– Peg Durkee, Coordinator, **Summerthing,** ***Boston City Hall***

"I've heard several times a voice like yours, a voice I want to be mine. It's such a tiny voice in education. So tiny, I've wondered if I could be wrong. I've found your voice today a little stronger and I wonder if it will ever be the voice of education – public education. I've got a long way to go to be the kind of teacher I want to be. But 'I know more than I think I know' and 'I can do more than I think I can do' and I will."

– Linda Shortman, Bloomingdale NJ public schools

"Truly, a document of 'revelations and adventures,' *Making Things* is an answer to the child's perpetual question, 'what can I do?' Also an antidote for the disease known as 'televisionitis,'...[it] encourages the reader to become adept in many skills and to gain a measure of self-understanding as he develops latent talents for creativity."

– J.J. Curto, Tallahassee (FL) **Democrat**

CONTENTS

Credits and Thanks vi
Dear Beginners and Late Starters vii
Permissions viii
The Animal School: A Parable ix
Learning by Doing xi
Save Things for Making Things xii

Paper Lace Hangers 2
More Paper Lace Hangers 4
Star Balls 4
Paper Sculptures 5
Paper from Vegetable Fibers 6
Paper-Making Master Notes 8
Kiko's Seagull 10
Flapping Owl 11
Fold & Cut 12
3-D Stand-up Scenes 13
Paper Beads 14
Paper Curls & Mobiles 16
Tissue Fish 17
Paper Glider 18
Paper Spinners 19
Paper Faces 20
Finger Puppets 22
Paper Bag Puppets 23
Corrugated Cut-Away 24
Printing Fingers 25
Printing Vegetables 26
Printing Potatoes 28
Block Printing 30
Roller Printing 32
Fish Printing 33
Marbleized Paper 34
Smoke Paper 35
Bookmaking 36
Binding Signatures 38
Cloth Book Jackets 40
Butterfly Book 42
City Book 43
Clay Leaves 44
Pasta Beads & Paper Clips 45
Finger Painting 46
Crayon Activities 47
Marionettes 48
Slotted Animals 50
Climbing Pull Toys 51
Tin Lid Ornaments 52
Hammered Wire Jewelry 53
Balancing Toys 54
Mobiles 56
Balancing Shapes 57
Straw Mobile 58
Salt Pendulum 60
Bed Friends & Ummm-Dears 62
Pillow Cozies 63
Mouse Pouch 64
Appliqué & Stitchery 65
Stitches 66
Rug Hooking 68
Portable Houses 70
Box Houses 71
Box Horses 72
Cardboard Racing Turtles 73
Stilts 74
The Wire Hanger 76
Camping Aids 78
Grass Hats, Mats, Sacks, and Soles for the Feet 80
Animated Motion 82

Zoetrope	83
Kites	84
Plastic Bag Sled Kite	85
Twisting	86
Rope Winding	87
Over & Under Weaving	88
Plastic Drinking Straw Belt Loom	89
The Heddle	90
Popsicle Stick Heddle Loom	91
Box & Stick Inkle Loom	92
Thrumming Loom	94
Weaving in Math Class	96
Weaving Patterns	98
Weed Weaving	99
Twining	100
Macramé Knots	102
Macramé Belt	103
Macramé Necklace Sampler	104
Love Pouch	105
Knots	106
Commando's Vest	108
Quick Clothes	110
Body Logic Clothes	112
Donut Blouse	114
Tie-Dye	116
Dyeing	117
Quick Batik	118
Stocking Masks	120
Braid Wig	121
Glove Finger Puppets	122
Odd Sock Puppets	123
Soap Mitten	124
Ivory Soap Boat	125
Soap Sculpture	125
Giant Bubbles	126
Go Fish	128
Xylophone	130
Sweet Sounds from Found Objects	131
Candle Casting	132
Candle Dipping	134
Energy Toys	135
Box Costumes	136
Box Sculptures	136
Window Shade Maps & Murals	137
Stained Glass Cookies	138
Bread Dough Sculptures	140
Peaceable Bread	142
Casting Plaster	144
Sand Casting	145
Plaster Scrimshaw	146
Plaster Carving Blocks	147
Connecting Things with Ideas	149
Questions	150
Solutions	151
The Making of _Making Things_	152
Art and Craft Books	156
Books on Ways of Learning	157
Index	158

CREDITS AND THANKS

The ideas for this book came from my childhood at two progressive schools, The City & Country School and The Little Red School House, both in Greenwich Village, New York, where we learned by doing in the spirit of John Dewey's philosophy. Many thanks go to my parents and grandparents, who were all creative in different ways. My growing-up years in New York City gave me access to some very gifted and unique people such as Dorothy Coit and Edith King, who ran the King-Coit Children's Theater, where the arts were wonderfully demonstrated. I studied at the Art Students League and worked at the Museum of Modern Art, Victor D'Amico's People's Art Center, and Lord & Taylor's in the window display department, immersed in creative process.

While I was program director at Mike Spock's wonderful hands-on museum for children in the early formative days in Jamaica Plain, Massachusetts, I had lots of visitors to test these ideas on and lots of creative people to work with, such as Allan Conrad, Maury Segoff, Phillis Morrison, Clara and Bill Wainwright, Cynthia Cole, and Bernie Zubrowski; also people at the Educational Development Center, the Workshop for Learning Things, and innovators such as George Cope, John Merrel, and Nat Burwash. Thanks to Michael Grater for the paper face; to Louise Tate, who was director of the Massachusetts Council for the Arts and Humanities, which sponsored my move to Boston in 1968; to Dr. Alice Baumgartner, director of the New Hampshire Commission on the Arts, which sponsored my Making Things workshops for elementary-school teachers.

Thanks to my boys, Piet and Kiko, who helped me grow up and who got good at all these skills before leaving home to build their own houses.

Thanks to the Michael Karolyi Foundation, in Vence, France, for a fellowship and the time to draw these pages.

DEAR BEGINNERS AND LATE STARTERS

Remember, you know more than you think you know. And what you learn now in your early years will last longer and be firmer in your memory bank than anything else you learn later.

When you have tried most of the activities in this book, you will have taught your hands lots of useful skills for fun, for necessity, for leisure, and for survival.

These skills and concepts can set your imagination free and inspire you to try your own variations.

As you train your eyes to see and your hands to know, you will strengthen your belief in yourself.

Don't be afraid to ask questions and go beyond the rules.

Experiment in safety, and learn by doing.

"Play is very serious business,"
says Erik Erikson.

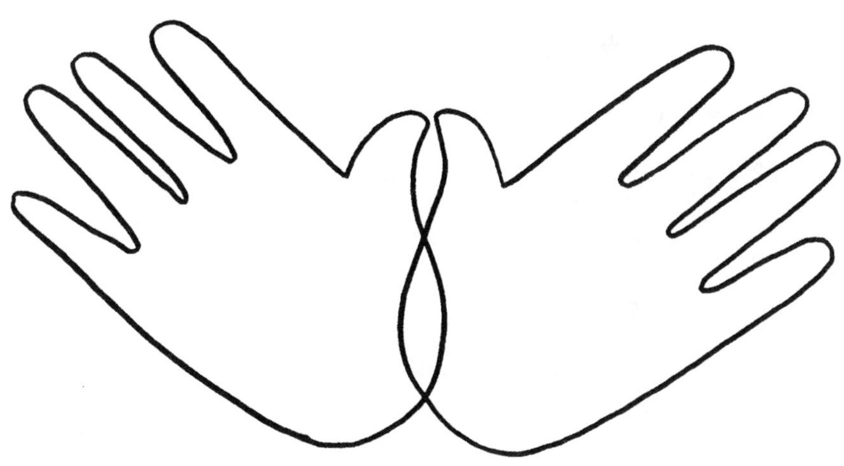

PERMISSIONS

It's OK to try something new.

It's OK to make mistakes.
You will learn a lot from them.

It's OK to take risks.

It's OK to take your time.

It's OK to find your own pace.

It's OK to try it your way.

It's OK to fail. You can always
try again free of fear.

It's OK to look foolish.

It's OK to be different.

It's OK to wait until you feel ready.

It's OK to experiment (in safety).

It's OK to question the "shoulds."

It's special to be you.

It is necessary to make a mess
—which you are willing to clean up.

The act of creation is often messy.

THE ANIMAL SCHOOL: A Parable

Once upon a time, the animals decided they must do something decisive to meet the increasing complexity of their society. They held a meeting and finally decided to organize a school.

The curriculum consisted of running, climbing, swimming, and flying. Since these were the basic behaviors of most animals, they decided that all the students should take all the subjects.

The duck proved to be excellent at swimming, better in fact, than his teacher. He also did well in flying. But he proved to be very poor in running. Since he was poor in this subject, he was made to stay after school to practice it and even had to drop swimming in order to get more time in which to practice running. He was kept at this poorest subject until his webbed feet were so badly damaged that he became only average at swimming. But average was acceptable in the school, so nobody worried about that — except the duck.

The rabbit started at the top of her class in running, but finally had a nervous breakdown because of so much make-up time in swimming — a subject she hated.

The squirrel was excellent at climbing until he developed a psychological block in flying class, when the teacher insisted he start from the ground instead of from the tops of trees. He was kept at attempting to fly until he became muscle-bound — and received a C in climbing and a D in running.

The eagle was the school's worst discipline problem; in climbing class, she beat all of the others to the top of the tree used for examination purposes in this subject, but she insisted on using her own method of getting there.

The gophers, of course, stayed out of school and fought the tax levied for education because digging was not included in the curriculum. They apprenticed their children to the badger and later joined the groundhogs and eventually started a private school offering alternative education.

— Alas, the author is unknown
(a student at the University of Toronto)

I hear
and I forget.

I see
and I
remember.

I do
and I
understand.

LEARNING BY DOING

The phenomenon of learning belongs to the child, not to the teacher. We do not teach a child to walk — one of many skill potentials in all beginners. At best, we stimulate discovery, desire, and curiosity; encourage and whet the appetite; provide space; and anticipate readiness to exercise the inevitable.

Learning by experience is profound knowledge, more deeply recorded in the memory than theory or speculation. The most direct, immediate, and satisfying path to knowledge is visual and manual experience linked with the urgency of interest.

Learning by doing connects products with ideas and history. It breeds creative thinking, self-expression, and originality, the confidence to experiment, and the courage to make mistakes, learn control, and perfect skills.

This collection of discoveries and resources is a careful selection of simple and important concepts that have shaped the cultures of the world. These activities should help to seed and develop natural curiosity and self-esteem. The projects are explained in pictures so that children just starting out and grown-ups who have missed out can quickly grasp the ideas.

Parents and teachers hold the success of children in their tone of voice and generosity of understanding. By encouraging self-discovery, by respecting originality and individualism, we avoid the preoccupation with competition, allowing students to progress at their own pace. Creativity is the birthright of all children. Let us foster it rather than cramp or nip it in its most eager time for learning.

SAVING THINGS FOR MAKING THINGS

Save:	**For:**
Egg Cartons	seed growing, lanterns, and sorters
Plastic containers	storage and weaving frames
Baby food jars	storage, sorters, bead keepers, and paints
Plastic straws	looms, construction, gliders, and more
Styrofoam meat trays	paper making, printing, and mobiles
Shoe boxes	sand casting, dioramas, looms, and silk screening
Old lamp shade wire	tubular macramé, bubble frames, and mobiles
Wood scraps	looms, block printing, carving, and building
Shirt cardboards	looms, slotted animals, and turtles
Buttons and beads	macramé, stringing, and games
Nuts and berries	stringing, games, and planting
Empty thread spools	ink stamps and pull toys
Tire inner tubes	relief patterns for roller printing
Magazines	collages, mosaics, and paper beads
Sticks and dowels	inkle looms, kites, and paint stirrers
Tongue depressors	hole-and-slot heddle looms
Toothpicks	construction
Old window shades	"wall-windows" and roll-up murals and maps
Fabric scraps	rug hooking and braiding and rag tapestries
Tin cans and lids	ornaments and lanterns
Colored telephone wire	jewelry, weaving, and sculpture
Gallon tin cans	foot raisers, templates, and lanterns
Milk cartons	bathtub boats, bird feeders, and planters
Refrigerator boxes	walk-in houses and puppet theaters
Nylon stockings	puppets, see-through masks, and weaving
Odd socks and gloves	hand and finger puppets
Gallon mayonnaise jars	moss gardens and batik dye savers
Clothespins	dolls and box animal legs
Wire clothes hangers	bubble frames and stocking mask frames
Soup bones	scrimshaw scratching and napkin rings
Chicken bones	cut bone beads

ETC. * ETC. * ETC. * ETC. * ETC. * ETC. * ETC.

This book is
dedicated to
the opposable
thumb

Making Things

PAPER LACE HANGERS

SQUARE

YOU WILL NEED:

HEAVY PAPER
PENCIL
RULER
SCISSORS
PAPER CLIP
THREAD

1. Use a square of paper any size.
2. Fold it corner to corner.
3. With open end facing down, draw $\frac{1}{4}$" margins along left and right sides.
4. Draw cutting lines as shown.

5. Cut in from left side to margin on right, then from right side to margin on left, etc.

6. Open folds carefully while paper is on the table.
7. Then pull tip up. Attach paper clip and thread, and hang it from a high place.

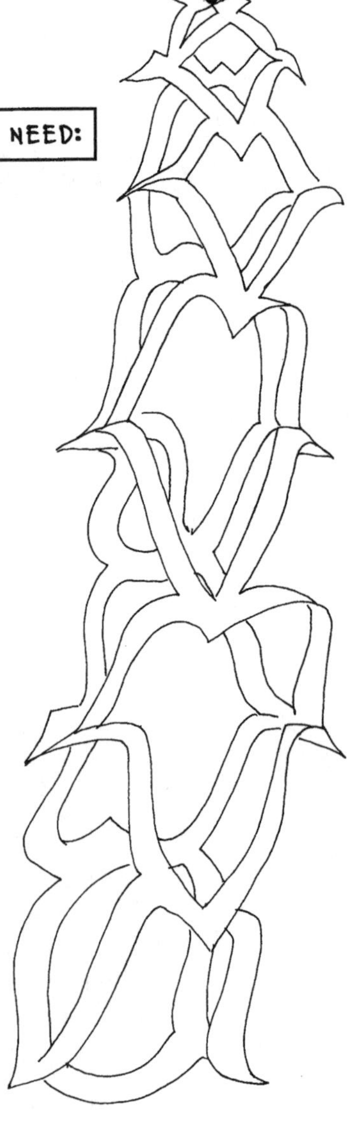

ROUND

1. Cut a round piece of paper. (You can trace a dish to draw a circle.)

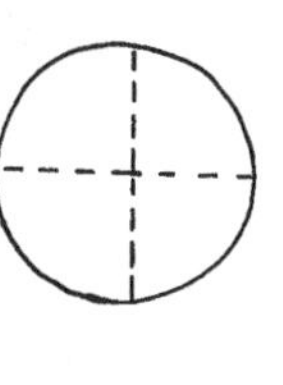

2. Fold it in half, then in half again.
3. With open end facing down, draw $\frac{1}{4}$" margins along left and right sides.

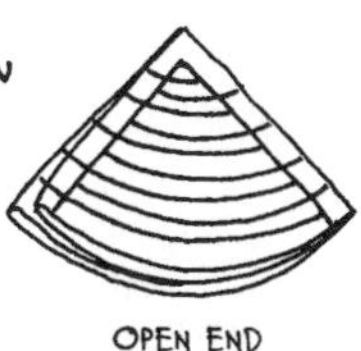

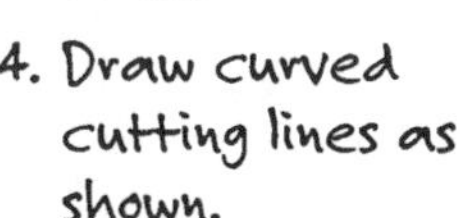

4. Draw curved cutting lines as shown.

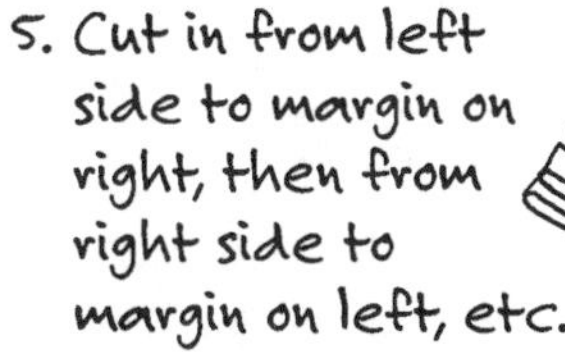

5. Cut in from left side to margin on right, then from right side to margin on left, etc.

6. Open folds carefully while paper is on the table.
7. Then pull tip up. Attach paper clip and thread, and hang it from a high place.

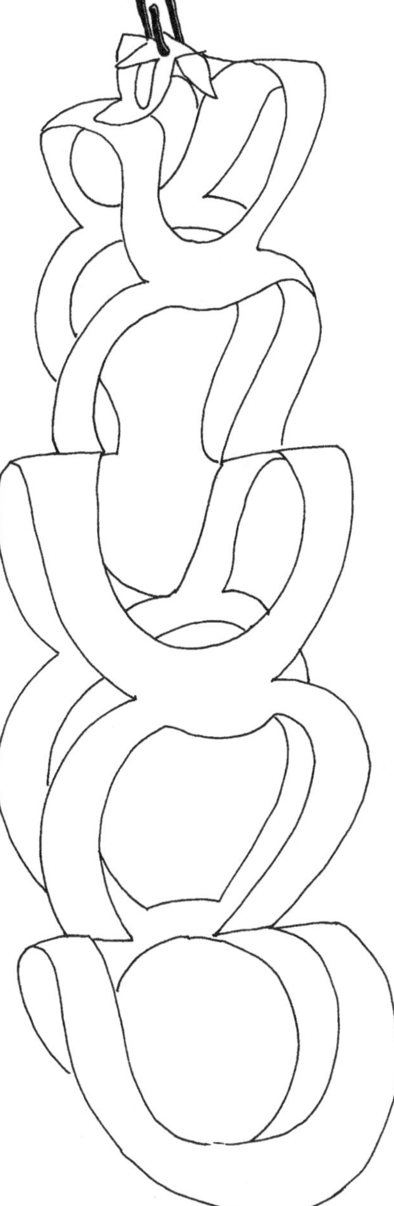

MORE PAPER LACE HANGERS

CIRCLE

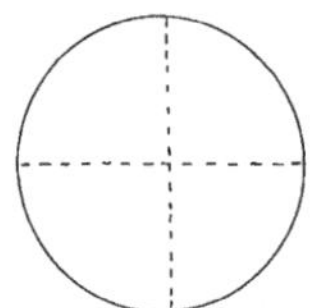

1. Fold a paper circle in quarters.

2. With double-fold side down, cut along dotted lines, stopping at margin.

3. Bend one moon left and one moon right.

OBLONG

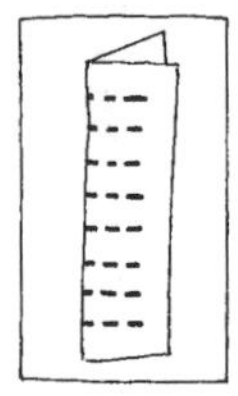

1. Fold a paper rectangle in half.

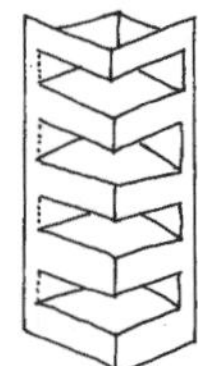

2. Cut to margin.
3. Bend one strip in and one strip out.

STAR BALLS

YOU WILL NEED:

COLORED PAPER • SCISSORS • PAPER CLIP

1. Cut out 7 paper disks.
2. Fold all but one in half.
3. Cut a slit about halfway in at center of each folded disk.
4. Slip cut disks onto flat disk.
5. Attach a paper clip hanger.

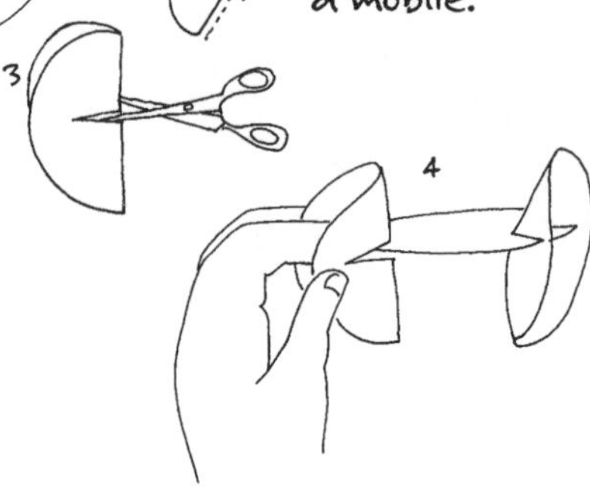

Variations

Cut: triangles, curls, odd shapes.
Combine several ornaments to make a mobile.

Try large and small ornaments.
Make up your own weird constructions.

PAPER SCULPTURES

PAPER RING SCULPTURES

YOU WILL NEED:

PAPER • SCISSORS • GLUE OR STAPLER • CRAYONS OR MARKERS

Experiment with cutting out a shape and then gluing or stapling the ends together in a ring. Add details with crayons or markers.

PAPER CONE BIRD

YOU WILL NEED:

PAPER • SCISSORS • GLUE • STAPLER (OPTIONAL) • PENCIL • MARKERS

1. Cut out and glue or staple a paper cone.
2. Cut out triangles for beak and wings. Cut a slit into bottom edge as shown. Fold along dotted lines, and glue tabs to bird body.
3. Cut strips, and curl ends around pencil. Glue them on for head and tail feathers.
4. Add details with markers, paper shapes, or by snipping into cone and folding out the cut-out shapes.

PAPER FROM VEGETABLE FIBERS

1. Make 2 wooden frames the same size (any size that fits in a dishpan). Staple a piece of window screen onto one frame. This is your <u>mold</u>; the other frame is your <u>deckle</u>.

2. Cut dry vegetable fibers into bits.

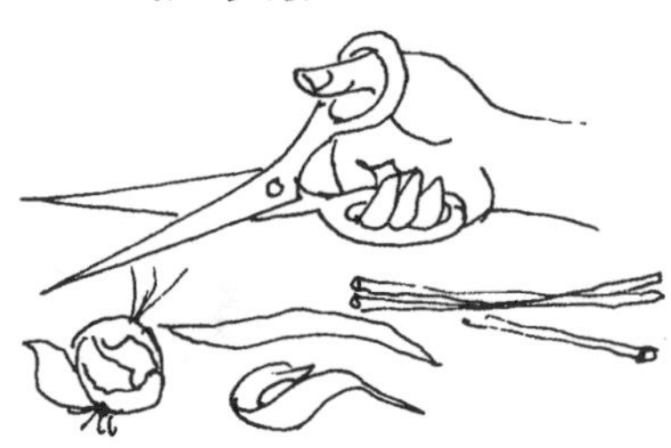

3. Put them in a blender, then add a torn-up paper towel or other torn-up paper as filler. Fill blender with water, and blend until smooth. This is called <u>slurry</u>.

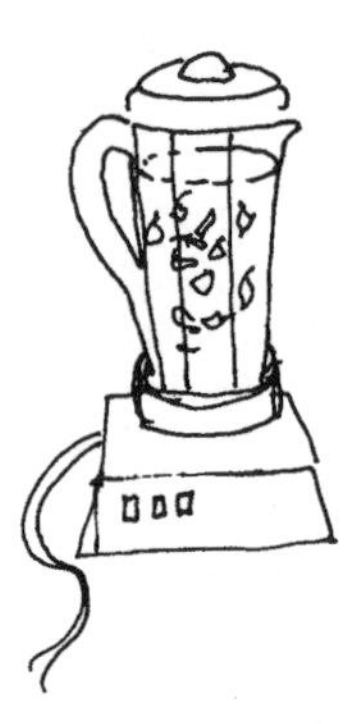

4. Partially fill dishpan with water, and pour in slurry. Position the mold screen side up, and place the deckle on top of it.

5. Holding the mold and deckle tightly together, dip them into the slurry.

6. Holding them level, raise mold and deckle horizontally. Allow water to drain, leaving mash undisturbed on screen. This is called a <u>wet leaf</u>.

YOU WILL NEED:

8 STRIPS OF WOODEN LATH (OR CUT A WOODEN YARDSTICK) • SMALL NAILS • HAMMER • WINDOW SCREENING • STAPLE GUN • DRY VEGETABLE FIBERS, SUCH AS CORN HUSKS, ONION SKINS, CELERY STRINGS, SAWDUST, WEEDS, OR STRAW • SCISSORS • BLENDER • PAPER TOWELS, NAPKINS, PAPER BAGS, NEWSPAPER, OR TISSUE • DISHPAN • NEWSPAPER • SPONGE • IRON

7. Set mold and deckle down on a sheet of newspaper, and remove deckle.

8. Place a newspaper sheet on top of the wet leaf, to act as a blotter.

9. Turn mold and newspaper blotter over, and put them facedown on table.

10. Sponge away excess water through screen.

11. Carefully lift mold up off the wet leaf.

12. Put another newspaper blotter on wet leaf, and iron it dry. Remove blotters.

See how many kinds of paper you can make.

PAPER-MAKING MASTER NOTES

RECYCLING WASTE PAPER AND NATURE'S DRY FIBERS

- Don't use hard, tough fibers such as bark or wood chips unless you have time to first hammer, pound, and boil them into a soft pulp.
- For textured papers, blend reedy grasses into a slurry of paper towel, add pencil shavings or mashed egg carton into the blender, or press milkweed silk into a wet leaf made from brown paper bag or paper towel. Try laminating yarn scraps, ferns, or pressed lilac blossoms into a wet leaf. Emboss your paper by pressing a bent wire design into a wet leaf. Scraps of colored tissue or construction paper will add color to the slurry.
- If the slurry gets scrumpled on the screen, wash it off and dip again. Don't rearrange the slurry or wet leaf with your fingers because it will disturb the evenness of the sheet.
- Each sheet of paper gets progressively thinner as you dip. From time to time you will need to add more slurry to the bath.
- Don't pour slurry down the sink drain, unless you sieve it first. It is best to flush it down the toilet or pour it outside on the ground.
- Sizing is optional, but it makes paper less absorbent and easier to write on. Heat 1½ ounces of bone glue, hide glue, or gelatin and 1 pint of water until glue or gelatin is dissolved and smooth. Pour glue mixture into a pan or tub big enough to fit your paper. Add another pint of cold water to the mixture, and slide each sheet of dry handmade paper in and out of the sizing bath. Blot the paper with newspaper, and press it dry with an iron.

- Newspaper blotters sometimes leave print on your fresh paper sheets. If it is a problem, use paper towel blotters. Or if you are making many sheets or setting up a children's paper factory — as we did at the Boston Children's Museum, where sometimes 300 kids each made a sheet of paper per day — invest in several yards of white felt cut to the size of your frames, and use the felt pieces as blotters, squeezing them out between uses.
- A kids' paper-making factory is a great idea for Christmas or summer fairs. At the end of the paper-making table, set up a table with potato prints, letter stamps, Styrofoam shapes, and ink pads for printing greeting cards. Or set up a bookmaking table, and use textured handmade paper as endpapers in your hand-bound books.
- Reading and writing become much more exciting when you create your own books, telling and illustrating your own stories.

Paper is one of the most important and useful materials humans have ever created. Until a hundred years ago, paper was made by hand and was mostly used for precious documents.

Wasps taught us how to make paper. (Have you studied a hive?) Wasps chew fibers and weeds into a kind of paste or mash, then spit it out to form the walls and chambers of their hive; when it dries, it is a kind of paper sculpture.

The first people to make paper were the Chinese, in 105 A.D. In the sixth century, when the Chinese lost to the Arabs at the Battle of Samarkand, captured paper makers were forced to share their craft with their new masters. A thousand years later, the art of paper making reached Europe.

KIKO'S SEAGULL

AND OTHER BIRDS

YOU WILL NEED:

CARDBOARD OR HEAVY, STIFF PAPER SUCH AS OAK TAG • PENCIL • SCISSORS • CRAYONS OR MARKERS • THREAD

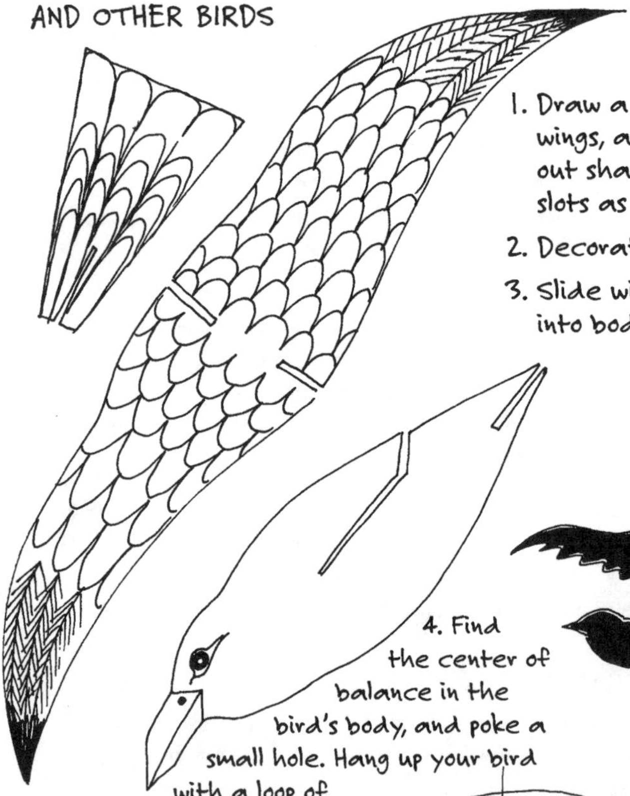

1. Draw a bird body, wings, and tail. Cut out shapes, and cut slots as shown.
2. Decorate bird.
3. Slide wings and tail into body slots.
4. Find the center of balance in the bird's body, and poke a small hole. Hang up your bird with a loop of thread.

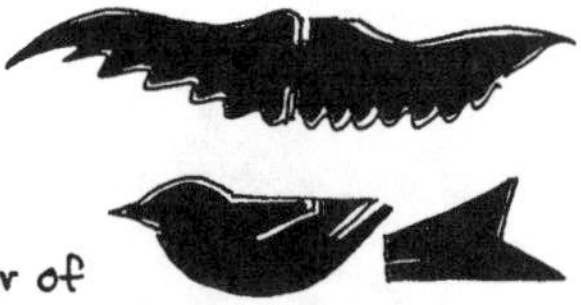

BASIC BIRD FORM

SWAN

Kiko found a seagull fledgling dying on the beach. Since he could not save its life, he drew it and gave it a second life.

FLAPPING OWL

YOU WILL NEED:

HEAVY CARDBOARD • PENCIL • SCISSORS • A HOLE PUNCH • CRAYONS OR MARKERS • STRING OR STRONG THREAD • 2 BRASS FASTENERS

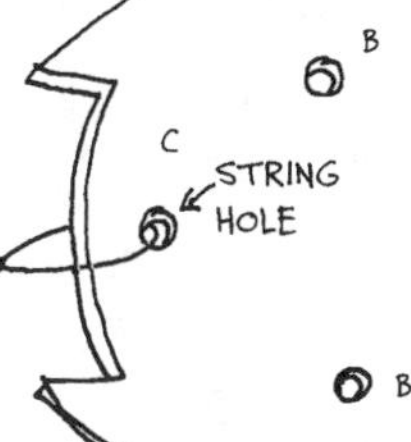

1. Cut out body and wings from cardboard.
2. Punch holes exactly as shown. Decorate owl with crayons or markers.
3. Knot a loop of thread onto the left and right wings at the A holes.
4. Attach wings to back of body by poking brass fasteners through the B holes. Push fastener ends down so wings are attached <u>very loosely</u> and can flap <u>easily</u> when you pull the string.

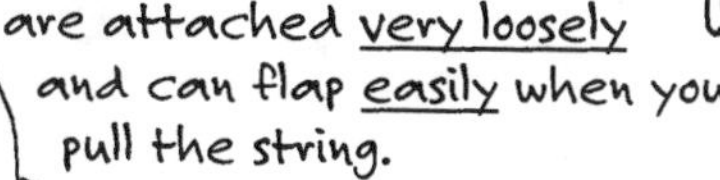

5. Tie a string at C, and hang owl in a doorway or on a wall hook near your bed.

FOLD & CUT

YOU WILL NEED:

PAPER OR CARDBOARD
(FILING CARDS WORK WELL.)
CRAYONS OR MARKERS
SCISSORS

FOLD

Cut along outline.

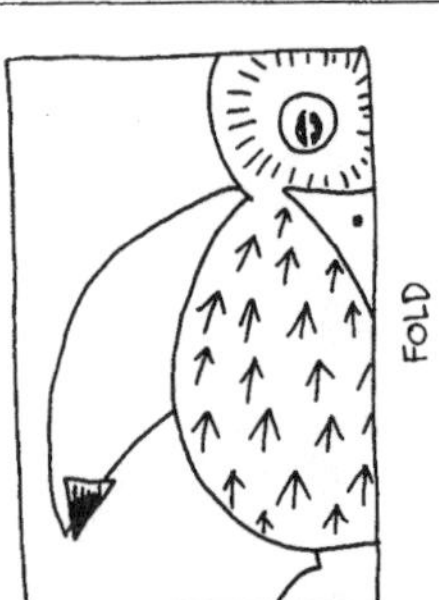

Draw figure on folded sheet. Note how the fold is used for standing the figure up. Cut around the image if you like.

FOLD IN 2

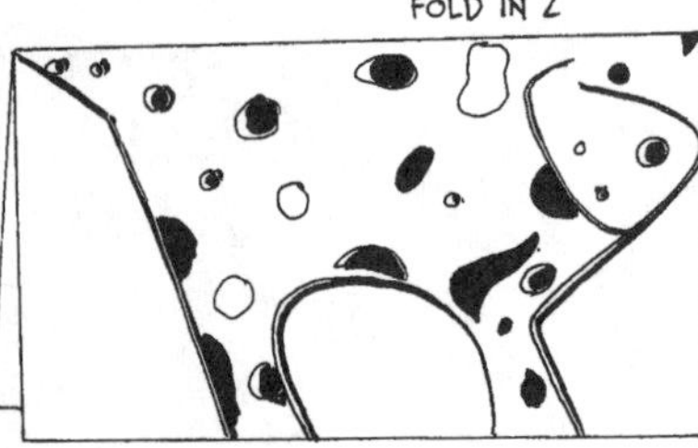

Good for stand-up letters, greeting cards, and place cards

3-D STAND-UP SCENES

YOU WILL NEED: CONSTRUCTION PAPER • CRAYONS OR MARKERS • SCISSORS

1. Draw a city, town, or village scene — trees, a pet, flowers, etc. — leaving space between each form.

2. Cut along the drawn lines except where things will bend (see dotted lines at right). (If you don't have good sharp scissors, put a folded sheet of newspaper under drawing and go over drawn lines with a sharp pencil until they cut through.)

3. Bend shapes up so everything is standing.

Good for dioramas, stage sets, Christmas cards, surprises, learning about perspective . . . and city planning

PAPER BEADS 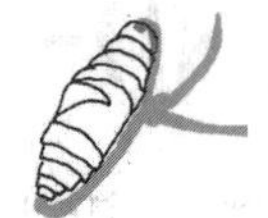

YOU WILL NEED: OLD MAGAZINES • PENCIL • RULER • SCISSORS • NAIL • WHITE GLUE • PAINTBRUSH • YARN OR THREAD

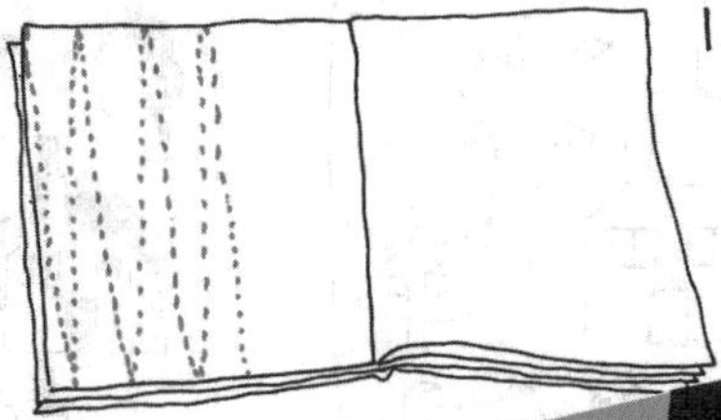

1. Choose a colored page fro
any magazine. Divide it int
wedges about 1" wide by
11" long.

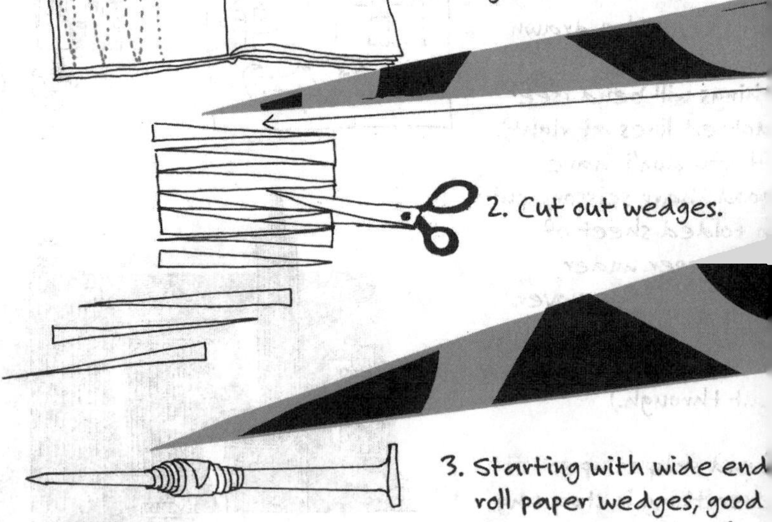

2. Cut out wedges.

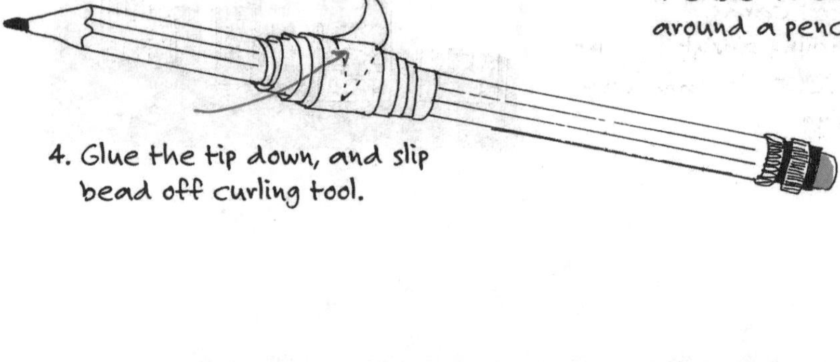

3. Starting with wide end
roll paper wedges, good
side out, around nail.
Small children may fin
it easier to curl wedge
around a pencil.

4. Glue the tip down, and slip bead off curling tool.

5. Paint the whole bead with glue, and let it dry. Then string beads on yarn or thread.

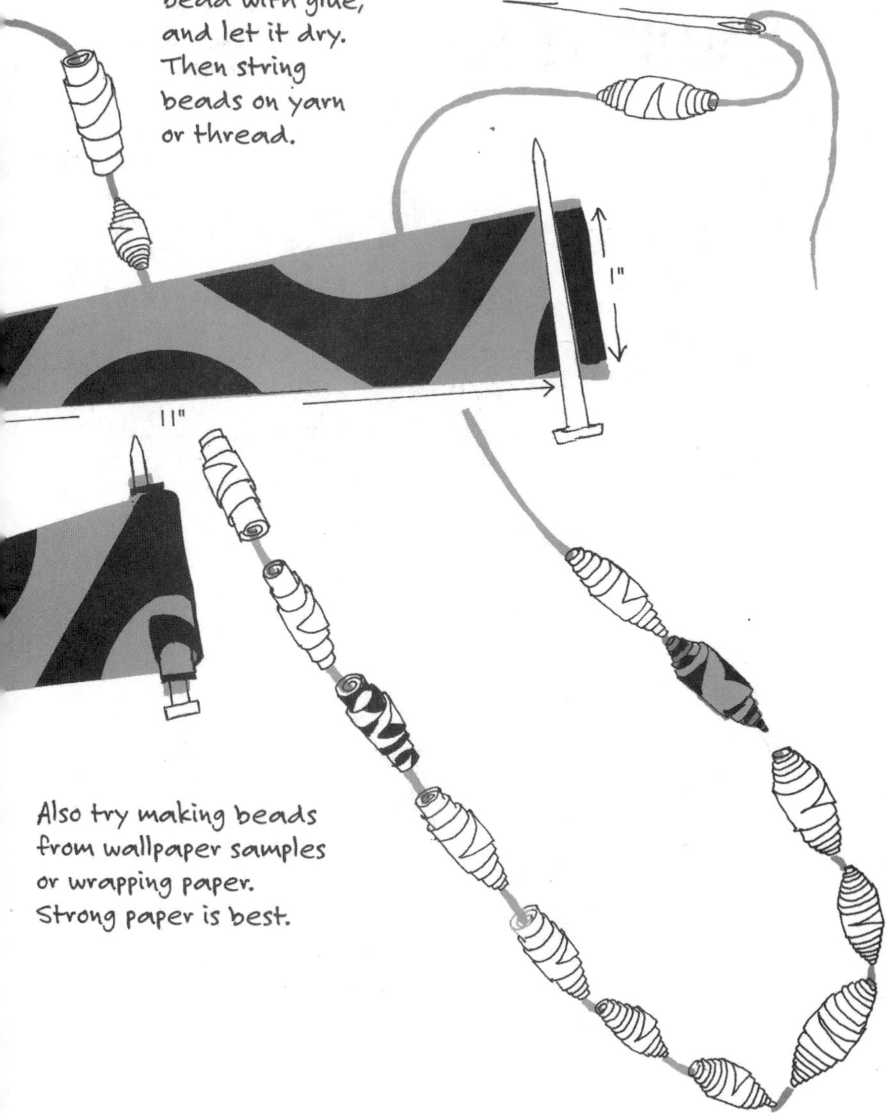

1"

11"

Also try making beads from wallpaper samples or wrapping paper. Strong paper is best.

PAPER CURLS & MOBILES

YOU WILL NEED:

CONSTRUCTION PAPER
SCISSORS
PENCIL OR NAIL
STAPLER

1. Cut paper strips — thick and thin, short and long.
2. Curl strips around pencil or nail.
3. Staple big and little loops.

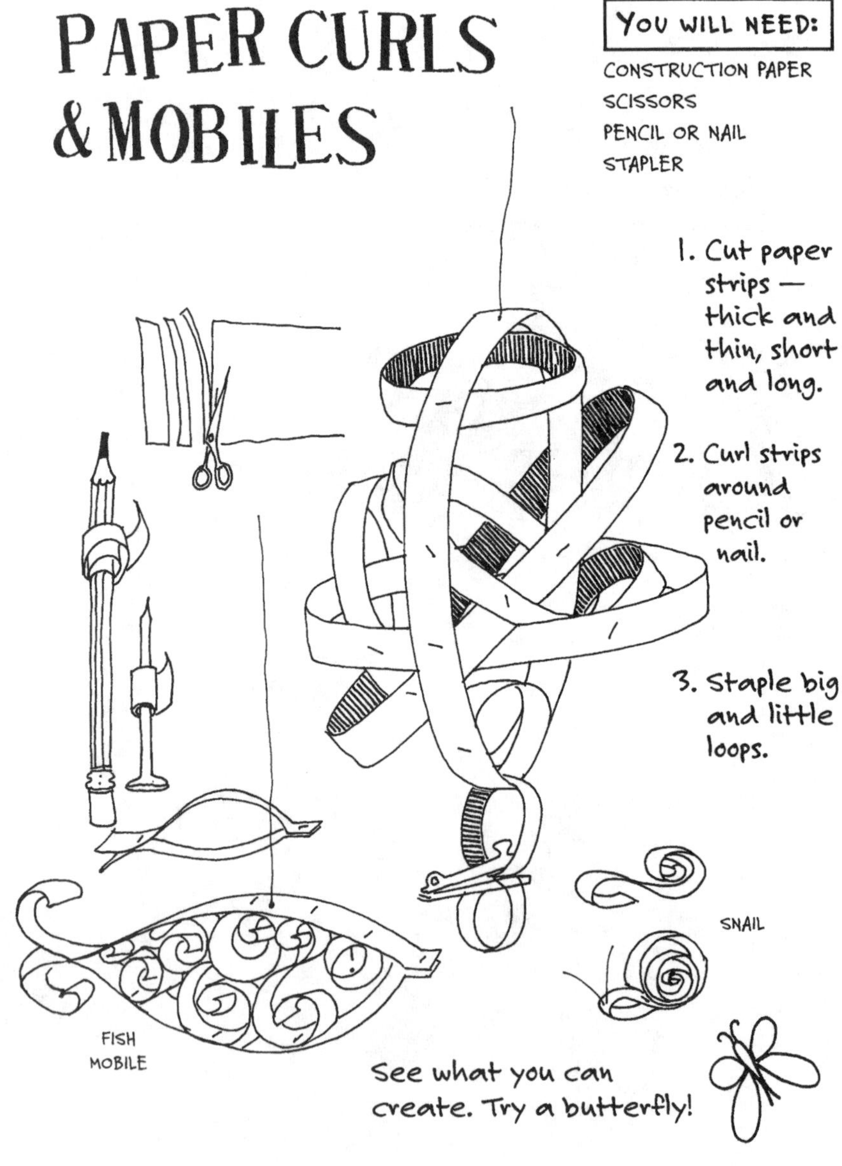

See what you can create. Try a butterfly!

TISSUE FISH

MOBILES FOR DRAFTY PLACES

YOU WILL NEED:

COLORED TISSUE PAPER
CRAYONS OR MARKERS
SCISSORS
GLUE
TOILET PAPER
THREAD

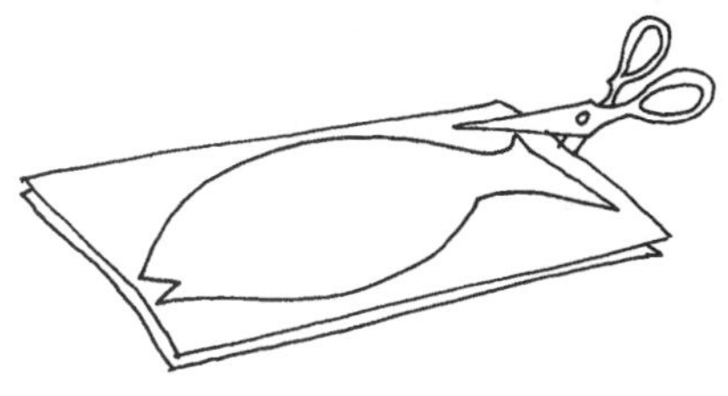

1. Draw a fish on double sheets of tissue paper, and cut shapes out.
2. Decorate your fish, and make fin shapes if you like.
3. Glue inside edges except for tail end.
4. When glue is dry, gently stuff fish envelope with toilet paper.
5. Find fish's center of balance, and hang up by thread.

PAPER GLIDER

YOU WILL NEED:

CONSTRUCTION PAPER • RULER • PENCIL • SCISSORS • 2 PAPER CLIPS • PLASTIC STRAW

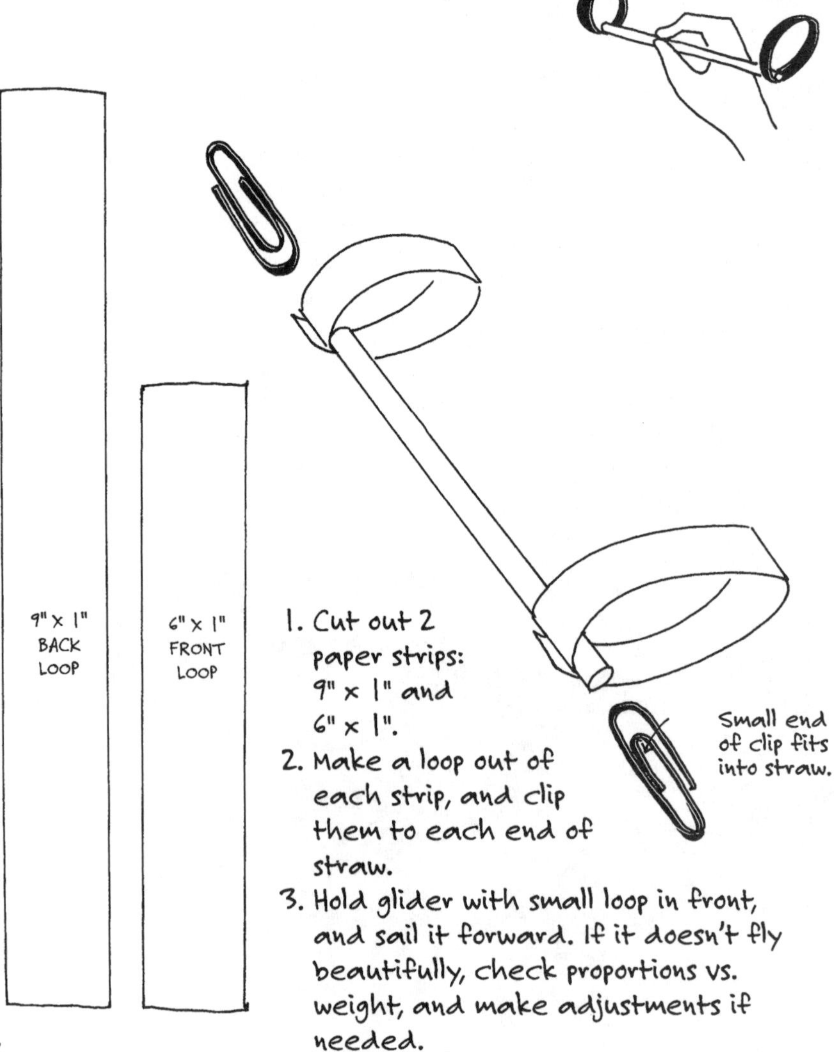

1. Cut out 2 paper strips: 9" x 1" and 6" x 1".
2. Make a loop out of each strip, and clip them to each end of straw.
3. Hold glider with small loop in front, and sail it forward. If it doesn't fly beautifully, check proportions vs. weight, and make adjustments if needed.

PAPER SPINNERS

YOU WILL NEED:

MEDIUM-WEIGHT AND LIGHTWEIGHT PAPER • RULER • PENCIL • SCISSORS • CARDBOARD • PIN

HELICOPTER

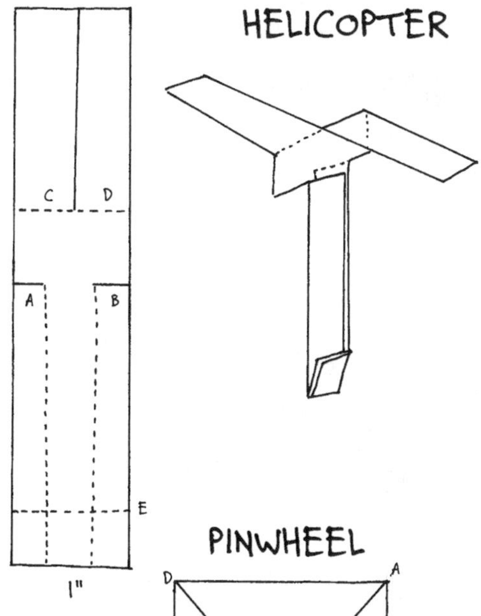

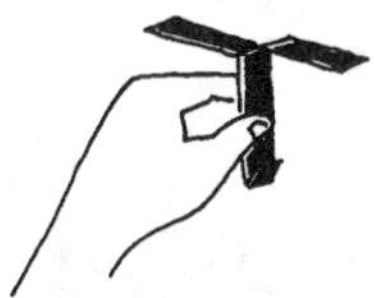

1. Cut out a strip of medium-weight paper about 4" x 1".
2. Cut along solid lines shown in diagram.

Fold A forward; fold B backward.

Fold C forward; fold D backward.

Bend stem at E.

3. Hold stem upright, and drop it from a high place.

Nature made the first spinners.

PINWHEEL

D A

CENTER

C B

1. Cut out a square of lightweight paper. Cut in from corners almost to center.

2. Cut out a small cardboard disk. Stick pin through center. Bend A, B, C, and D corners to center. Push pin into the 4 corners, into center, and into eraser of pencil. BLOW.

PAPER FACES

CAT
FAMILY
HUMAN
FAMILY
BIRD
FAMILY
BASIC
CAP
MOUSE,
DOG, AND
FOX
FAMILY

YOU WILL NEED:

PAPER
SCISSORS
CRAYONS OR MARKERS

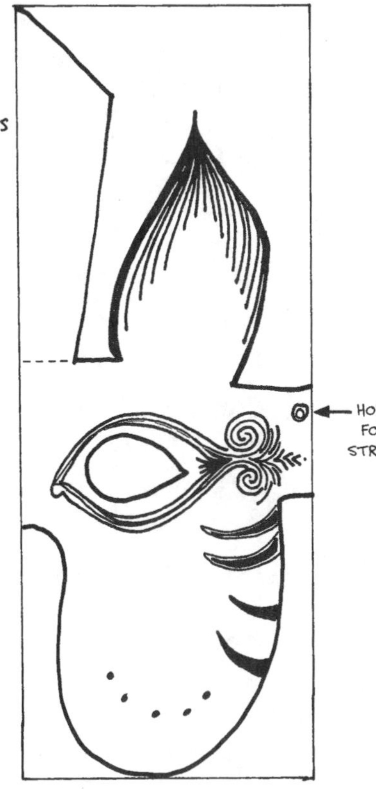

This is the nose or beak, which gets folded forward at dotted line.
HOLE FOR STRING

BASIC MASK

A sheet of office paper or construction paper folded the short way will fit the heads of both kids and adults.

Experiment until you develop some good designs.

Choose ear shape.

Choose nose shape.

Cut eye holes after measuring the distance from your nose.

Color nose on back of paper, because you fold it forward.

Add string to tie around your head.

EAR SHAPES

NOSE SHAPES

FINGER PUPPETS

YOU WILL NEED: FILING CARDS OR STIFF PAPER • CRAYONS OR MARKERS • SCISSORS

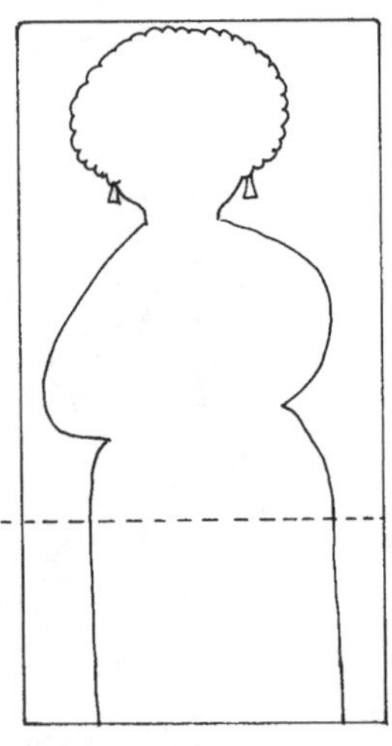

Fingers, fantastic fingers

1. Draw your puppet.
2. Cut out figure.
3. Cut holes to fit your fingers.
4. Fold finger section backward.
5. Put fingers through holes. Let fingers dance.

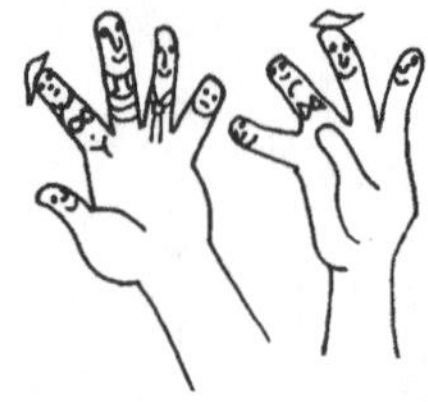

During a long automobile trip when we were children, a friend of my parents rode in the backseat with all the squabbling kids. She drew faces on her fingers and told us stories all the way. It was a wonderful trip, and we forgot to thank her.

PAPER BAG PUPPETS

YOU WILL NEED:

SMALL PAPER LUNCH BAG
CRAYONS OR MARKERS
COLORED PAPER
SCISSORS
GLUE
6"-DIAMETER PAPER PLATE
STAPLER (OPTIONAL)

Don't throw away your lunch bag; draw a puppet on it.

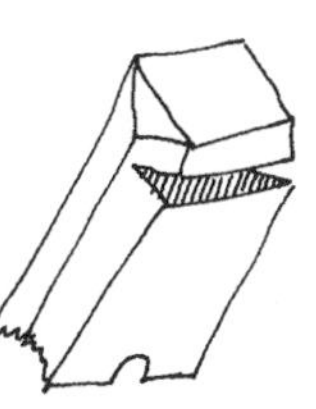

Cut a mouth opening.

For teeth, fold paper plate in half, and staple or glue it into opening.

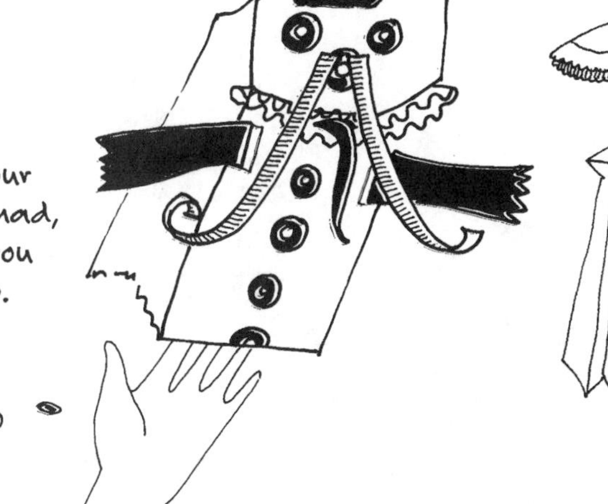

Decorate your puppet any mad, crazy way you can think up.

Put your hand inside, and tell us a story.

CORRUGATED CUT-AWAY

YOU WILL NEED:

CORRUGATED CARDBOARD (CUT-OFF SIDES OF A CARDBOARD BOX WORK FINE.) • PENCIL • X-ACTO KNIFE, MAT KNIFE, OR RAZOR BLADE

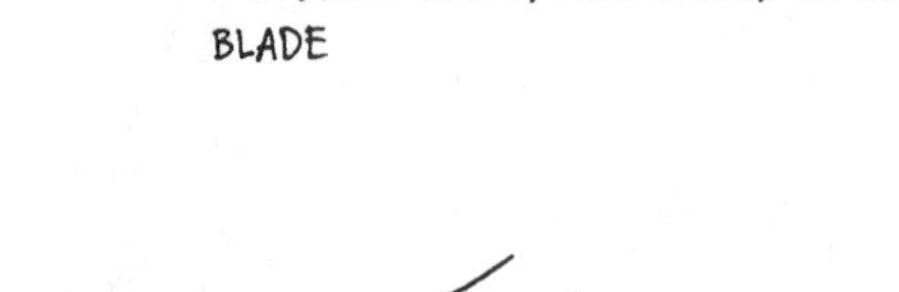

1. Sketch a design. If there is a choice, use the thin wall of the cardboard.
2. Cut into thin wall (not too deep).
3. Lift thin wall up off the corrugated humps. The trick is to coax the peel off one hump at a time. If wall is heavily glued, choose a less sturdy box.

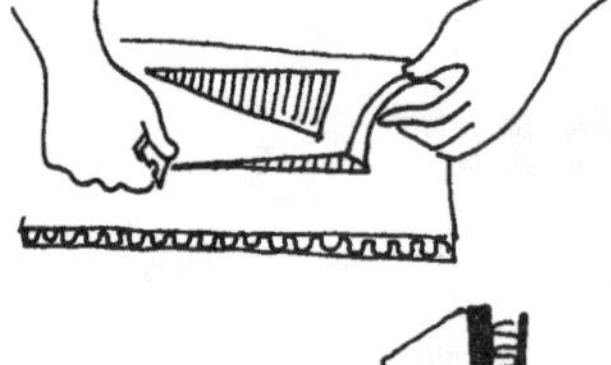

This project is for older children who can handle knives and razor blades.

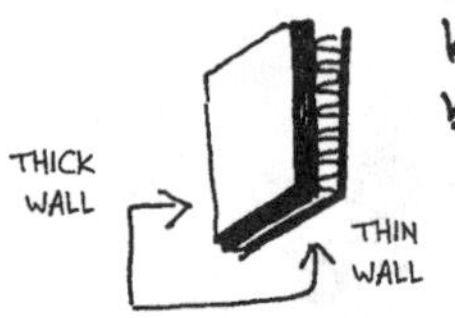

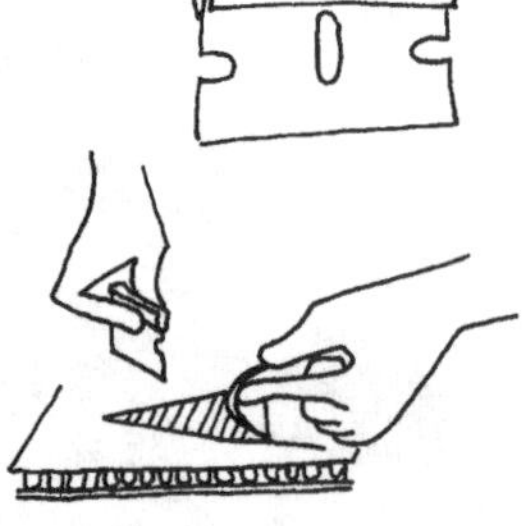

Note: Make simple shapes (wiggles and curls are difficult to cut).

CORRUGATED BLOCK PRINTS

Not only are cut-aways decorative as is, but you can also make prints from them. Roll the cut-away with linoleum ink. Press paper onto the inked surface, and peel off a print . . . or 10 . . . or 20.

PRINTING FINGERS

PRINTING VEGETABLES

AND THINGS

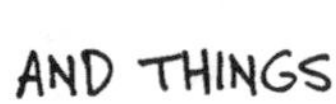

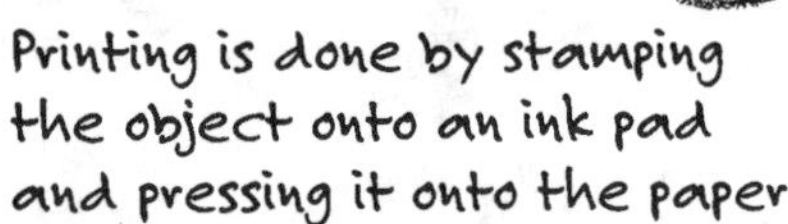

Printing is done by stamping the object onto an ink pad and pressing it onto the paper

OR by spreading ink on an object or relief surface, from which one can pull off a print. You can keep re-inking and pull off many prints.

YOU WILL NEED:

FRUITS AND VEGETABLES
KNIFE
INK PAD OR WATER-BASED LINOLEUM INK, COOKIE SHEET, AND ROLLER
PAPER

You can print:
- vegetables
- fruit
- fingers
- hands
- feet
- objects
- sponges

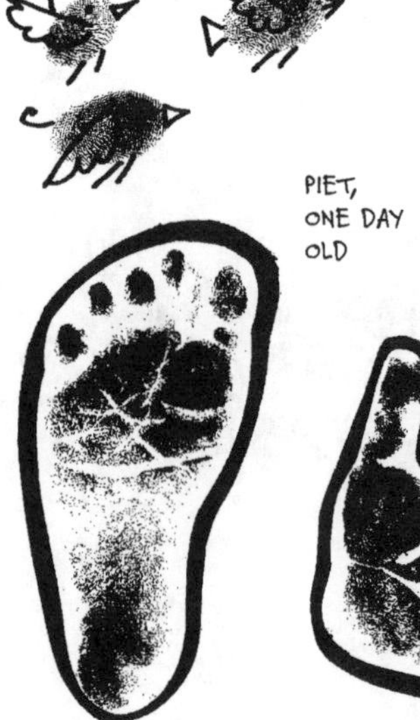

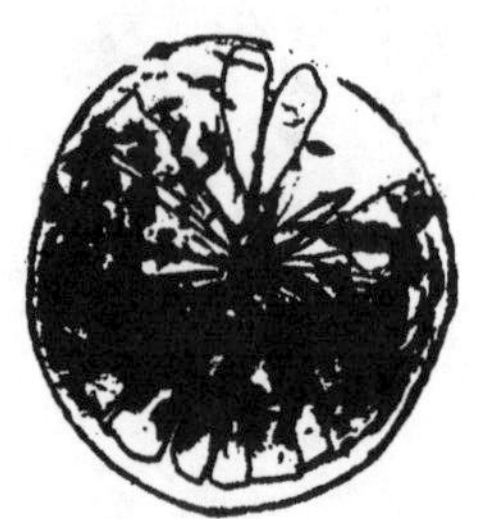

APPLE

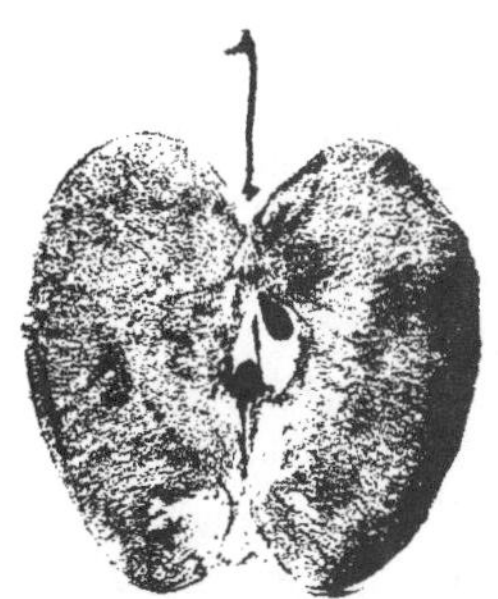

Cut fruits and vegetables in half to get interesting patterns.

ONION

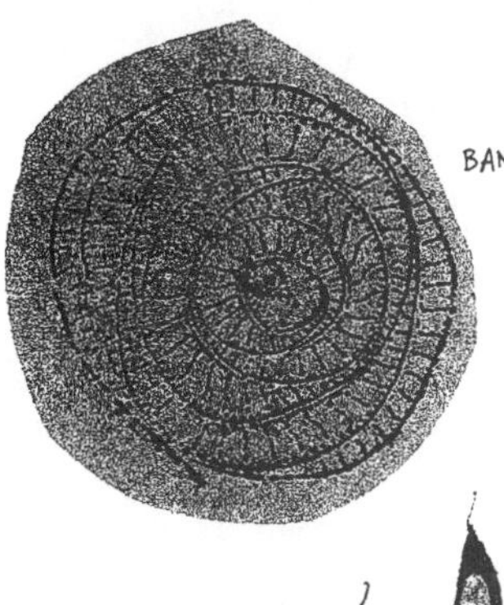

BANANA STALK

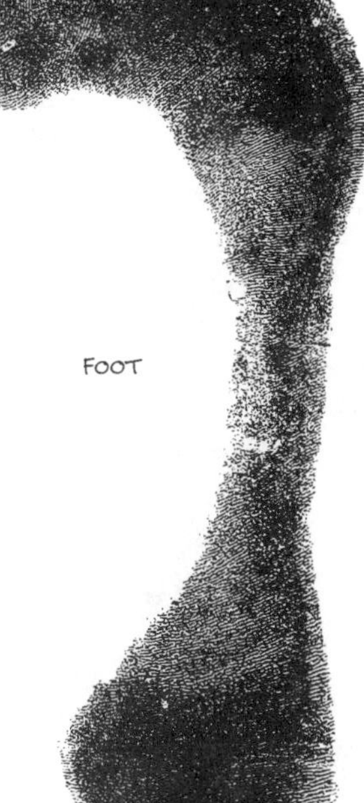

FOOT

STRING BEAN

PRINTING POTATOES

Potato printing is by far the easiest, most practical and economical printing method, especially for small people who don't use knives yet. For little kids, you can cut a collection of shapes to be used as stampers.

YOU WILL NEED: POTATOES • KNIFE • INK PADS; TEMPERA PAINT IN SAUCERS; OR WATER-BASED LINOLEUM INK, COOKIE SHEET, AND ROLLER • PAPER

See what you can make out of these basic shapes. Tack up a big piece of wrapping paper, or lay paper on the floor, and let everybody print, print, print, stamp, stamp, stamp.

Remember: Recognizable form is not what interests little kids at first. They just want to see what happens!

THIS OWL BUSINESS WAS ALL MADE FROM THESE SIMPLE SHAPES PUT TOGETHER.

Shapes can also be cut from carrots, turnips, and parsnips.

BLOCK PRINTING

YOU WILL NEED:

INK • COOKIE SHEET • ROLLER • PAPER
• ANY OF THE FOLLOWING:

WOOD	DESIGNS CAN BE ETCHED INTO WOOD SURFACE WITH LINOLEUM TOOLS.
LINOLEUM	COMES MOUNTED ON WOODEN BLOCKS OR IN SHEETS, EASILY ETCHED INTO WITH LINO TOOLS.
PLASTER	MADE IN FLAT PLAQUES, WHICH CAN BE SCRATCHED INTO AND USED FOR PRINTING
STYROFOAM MEAT TRAYS	DRAW OR SCRATCH INTO THEM WITH A PENCIL, PEN, OR PAPER CLIP — GREAT FOR LITTLE KIDS.
CORRUGATED CARDBOARD	CUT AWAY TOP LAYER; NO COST AND VERY INTERESTING.
GLUE OR STRING RELIEF	A RAISED LINE OF ELMER'S GLUE WHEN DRY OR STRING GLUED TO CARDBOARD CAN BE PRINTED.
COLLAGE RELIEF	CUT SHAPES FROM CARDBOARD OR INNER TUBES, AND GLUE THEM TO CARDBOARD.
SCRATCHBOARD	HAS A GESSO SURFACE, WHICH CAN BE SCRATCHED AND ETCHED.

All of these materials make good prints, and all can be printed in the following way using water-based or oil-based inks — though start with water-based; it's easier to clean.

1. Squeeze printing ink onto cookie sheet. Roll it out. Smooth it to cover roller.

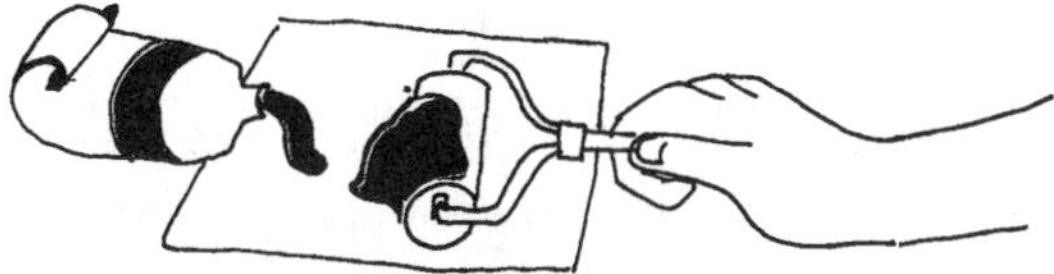

2. Roll ink over block evenly.

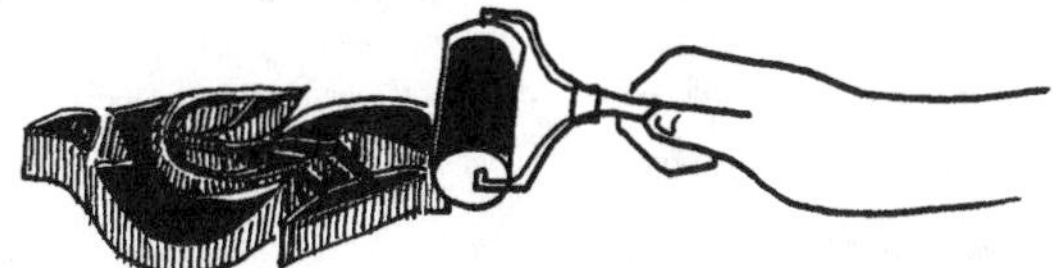

3. Press inked block onto paper, or press paper onto inked block. Rub gently. Peel paper back.

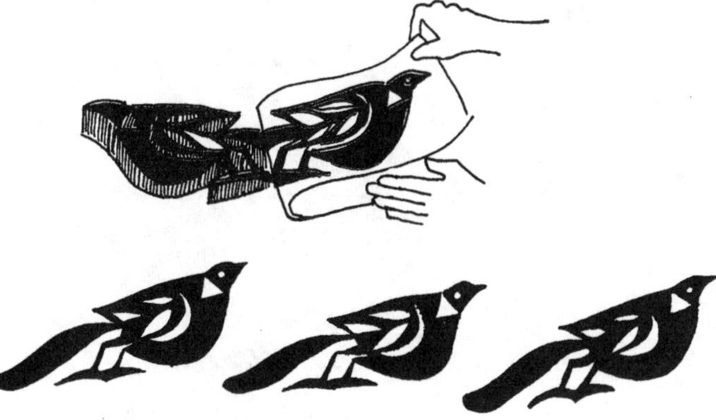

ROLLER PRINTING

Can be done with any cylinder that has been inked, painted, or pressed onto an ink pad and is then rolled out onto paper.

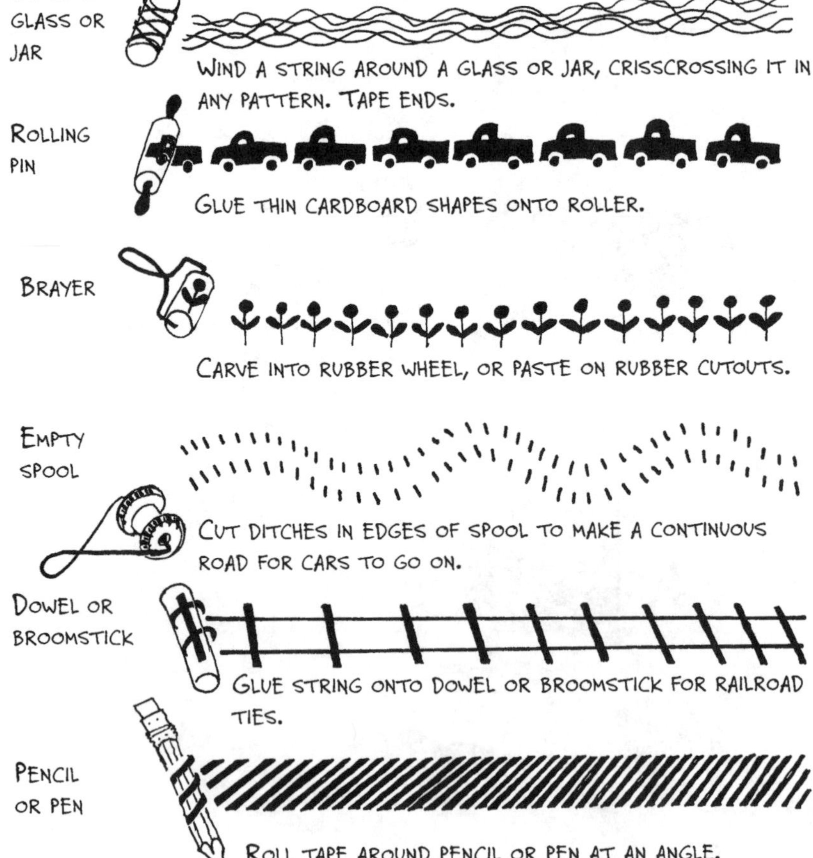

DRINKING GLASS OR JAR
WIND A STRING AROUND A GLASS OR JAR, CRISSCROSSING IT IN ANY PATTERN. TAPE ENDS.
ROLLING PIN
GLUE THIN CARDBOARD SHAPES ONTO ROLLER.
BRAYER
CARVE INTO RUBBER WHEEL, OR PASTE ON RUBBER CUTOUTS.
EMPTY SPOOL
CUT DITCHES IN EDGES OF SPOOL TO MAKE A CONTINUOUS ROAD FOR CARS TO GO ON.
DOWEL OR BROOMSTICK
GLUE STRING ONTO DOWEL OR BROOMSTICK FOR RAILROAD TIES.
PENCIL OR PEN
ROLL TAPE AROUND PENCIL OR PEN AT AN ANGLE.

FISH PRINTING

"Give me a fish and I eat for a day.

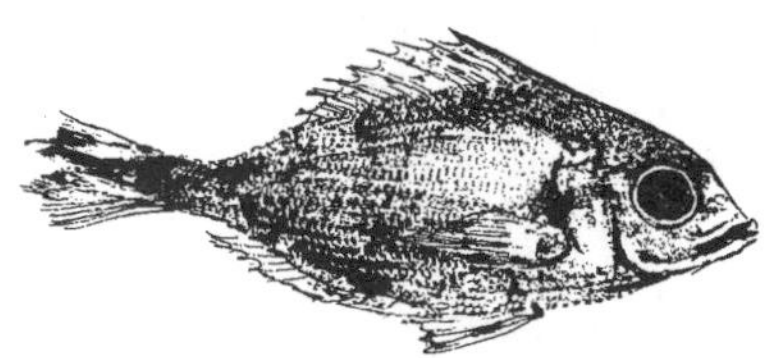

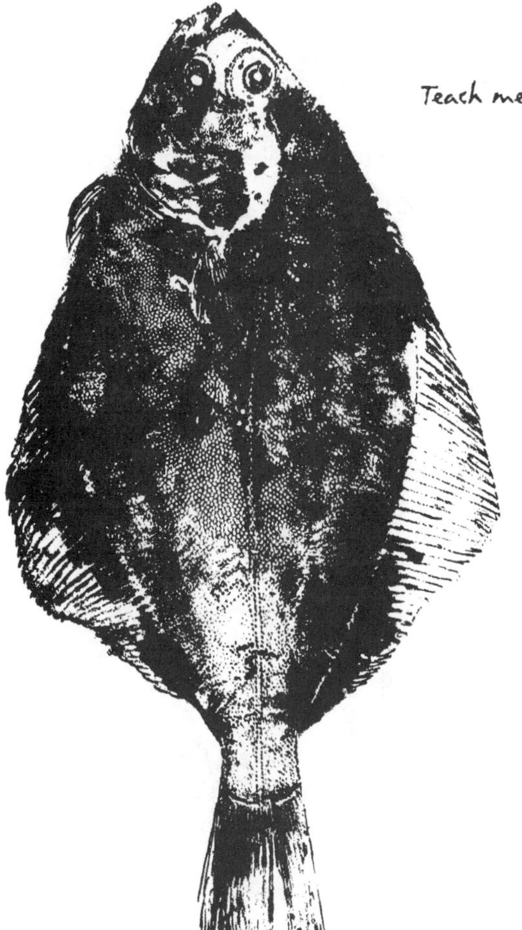

Teach me to fish and I eat for a lifetime."

This little flounder was inked and printed 300 times so 300 children from New Hampshire public schools could each have a "fossil print" to take home. Isn't he beautiful!

MARBLEIZED PAPER

YOU WILL NEED:

DISPOSABLE WATER PAN THE SIZE OF YOUR PAPER OR BIGGER
ENAMEL OIL PAINTS (2 OR 3 COLORS)
PENCILS
TOOTHPICK OR BROOM STRAW FOR STIRRER
PAPER

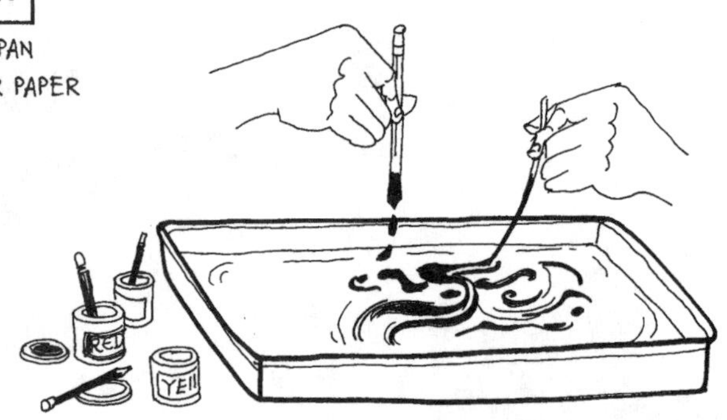

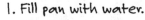

1. Fill pan with water.
2. Dribble paint off the pencil into the water, and gently swirl it around. Pull the oil drops into patterns.

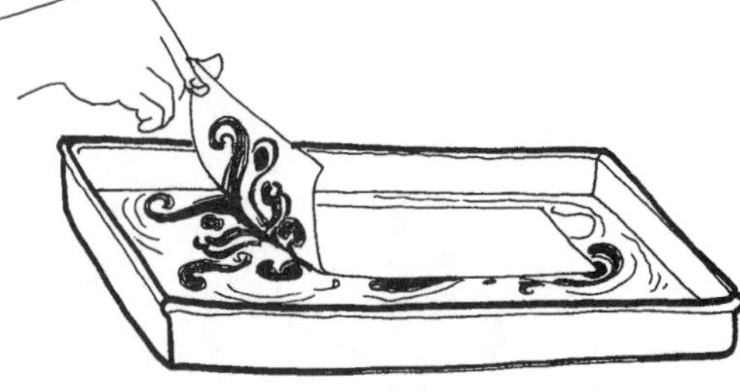

3. When you like the marbleized pattern, lay a sheet of paper on top of the design, then pick the paper up, lifting one corner and peeling it back slowly.
4. Allow sheet to dry overnight.

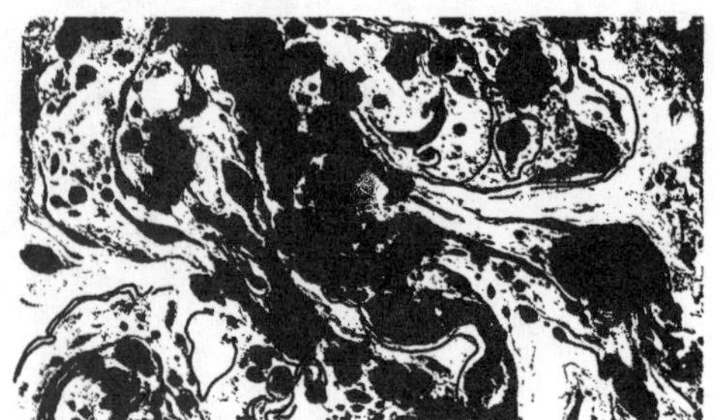

Marbleized paper makes beautiful endpapers or covers for your handbound books.

PAUL & NENA SERIOS'S

SMOKE PAPER

Write me a smoke letter

YOU WILL NEED:

DISPOSABLE WATER PAN THE SIZE OF YOUR PAPER OR BIGGER
BLACK INDIA INK
PENCIL
WHITE BOND PAPER
IRON AND NEWSPAPER (OPTIONAL)
ENVELOPES

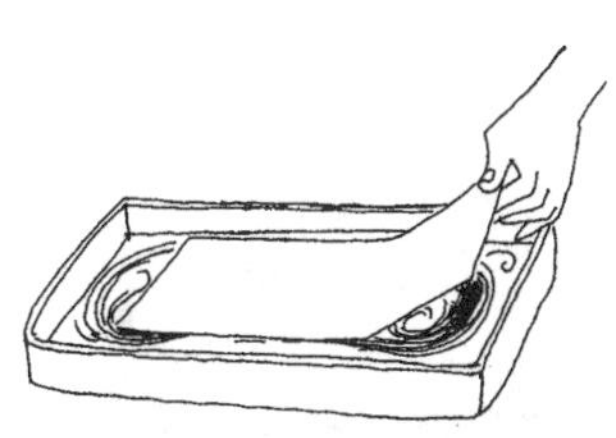

1. Fill pan with water.
2. Dribble india ink into water.
3. Gently swirl ink around with pencil.
4. Lay paper on top of design, then pull it up. (Don't soak paper for too long.)
5. Let dry. (Iron between newspaper sheets to help with drying if needed.)

BLACK

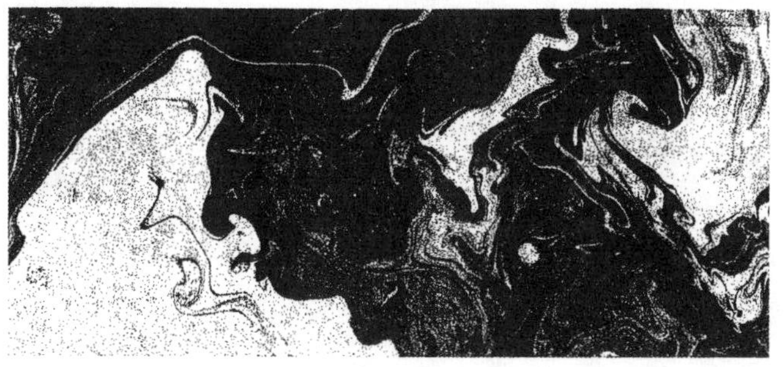

SIMPLE ONE-SIGNATURE

BOOKMAKING

YOU WILL NEED:

PAPER • SHARP NEEDLE • STRONG THREAD • CARDBOARD • SCISSORS • WHITE GLUE • WIDE TAPE

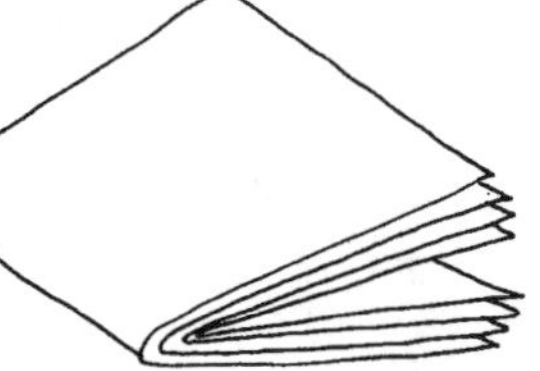

1. Fold 4 or more sheets of paper in half.
2. Use needle to poke 5 holes in folded sheets all at once so they line up well.
3. Sew from outside to center, leaving enough of a thread tail behind to tie a knot with later. Go in hole 1 and up through hole 2, in hole 3 and up hole 4, in hole 5 and back; up hole 4 and in hole 3, up hole 2 and tie thread ends together. These sewn sheets are called a <u>signature</u>.
4. Cut 2 pieces of cardboard $1\frac{1}{2}$" bigger than the pages on all sides except the rib side.

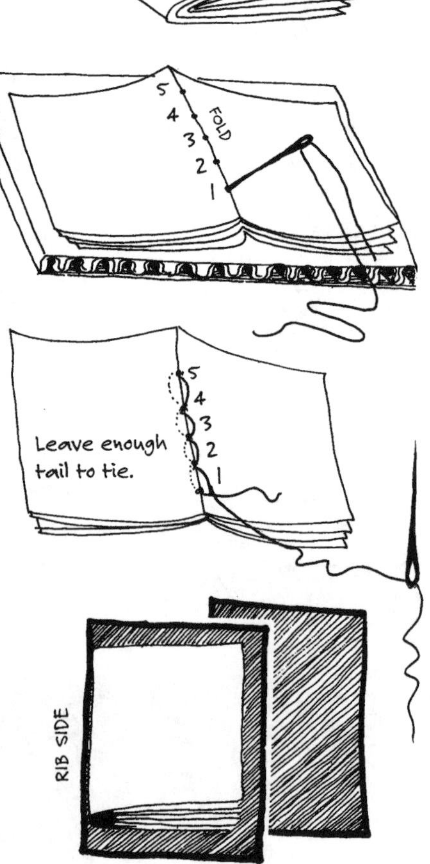

5. Cut 2 pieces of fabric or wallpaper 1" wider than cardboards except on rib side. Glue cardboard to inside of fabric or wallpaper. Glue corners down as shown, then edges.
6. Cut a strip of tape 3" longer than boards. Set boards $\frac{1}{4}$" apart onto sticky side of tape. Stick top and bottom of tape over onto boards.
7. Cover sticky rib with strip of paper.
8. Set pages into rib.
9. Holding boards at a right angle, glue first page to left board.
10. Holding boards at a right angle, glue last page to right board.
11. For endpapers, cut 2 pieces of paper and glue them inside front and back covers.

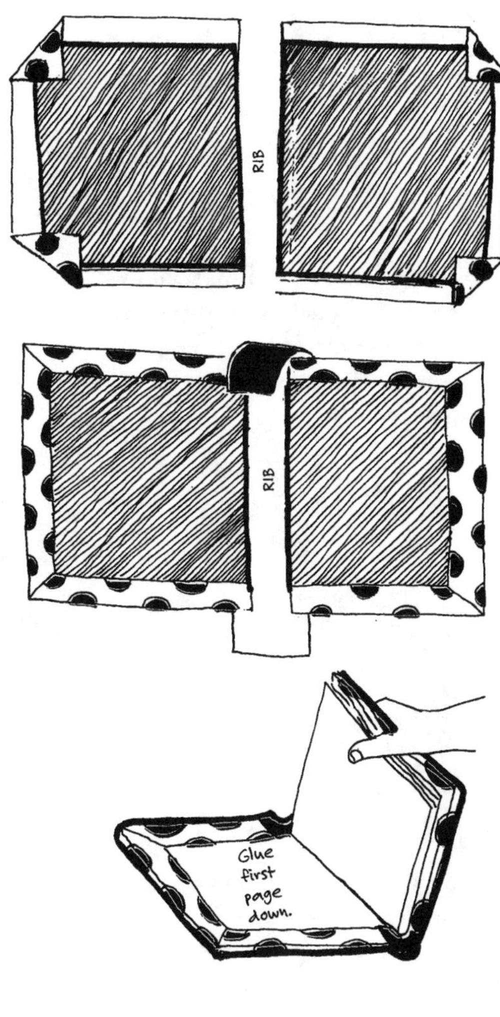

BINDING SIGNATURES

If you want to make a fat book, with more than one signature, you may either tape signatures together or sew them together and then bind with a cloth mull.

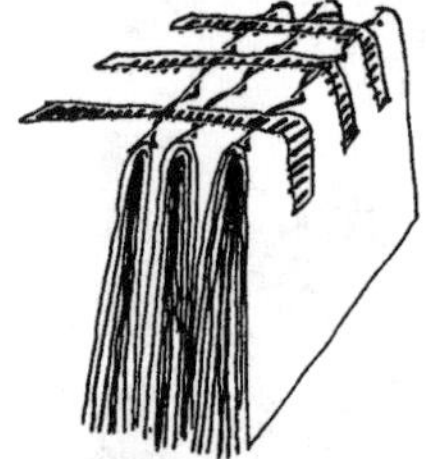

TAPING

Slip cotton strips or cotton tape under each set of sewing loops, and glue them down to front and back. (This method serves as a binding so you don't need a cloth mull.)

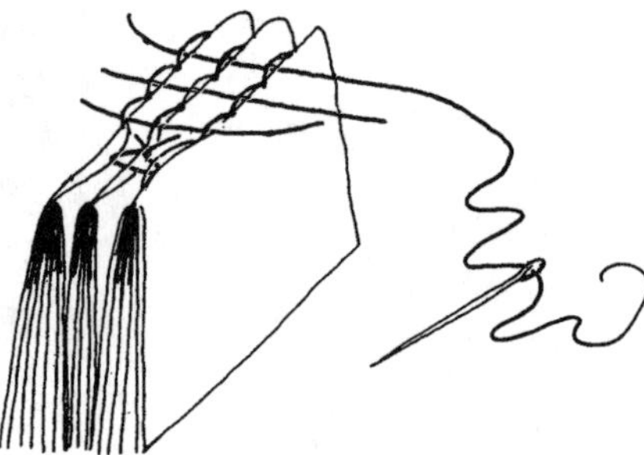

SEWING

CLOTH MULL

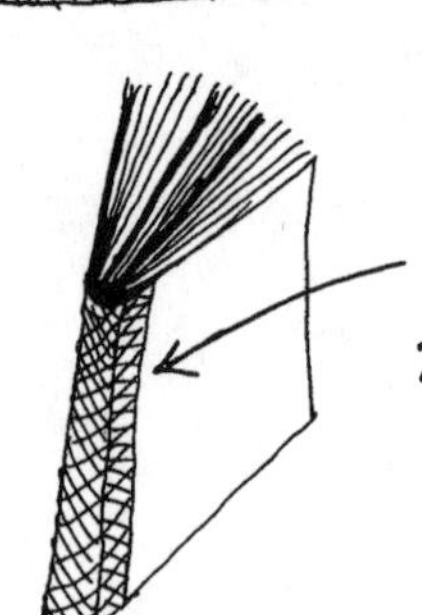

1. Slip thread under loops, and tie loosely.
2. Glue a strip of cotton (the mull) to the rib, tightly binding all the sewn signatures together.

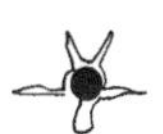

Once you have your signatures together, then follow the same process as earlier:

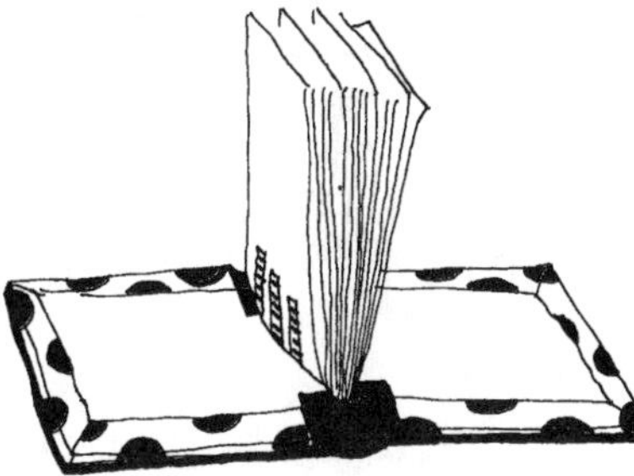

Set bound signatures into gutter folds of covered boards.

Glue front and back pages onto boards.

Add endpapers.

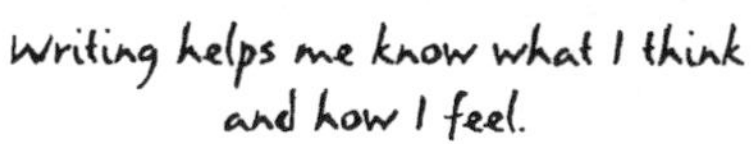

Writing helps me know what I think
and how I feel.

CLOTH BOOK JACKETS

YOU WILL NEED:

COTTON CLOTH
SCISSORS
PENCIL
THREAD OR YARN
NEEDLE

1. Cut cloth about 3" wider than your book all the way around.
2. Outline the book on the cloth so you know how far to cut the A flaps. Remove book.

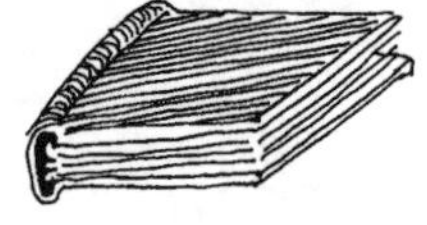

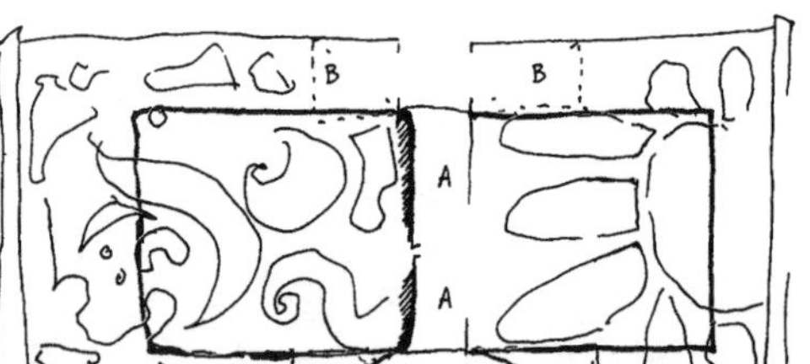

3. Cut A flaps, fold them inward, and put the book back in place.
4. Fold B corners as shown.
5. Fold bottom and top flaps over onto book boards. Sew from C to C and from D to D.
6. Fold outside flaps over.

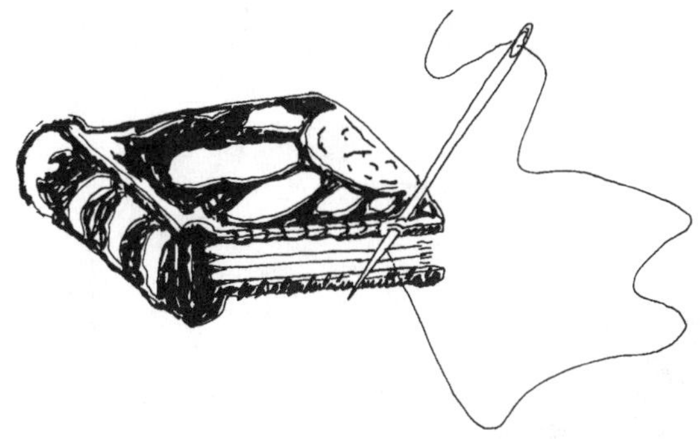

7. Close book, and sew edges (without sewing into the book!).

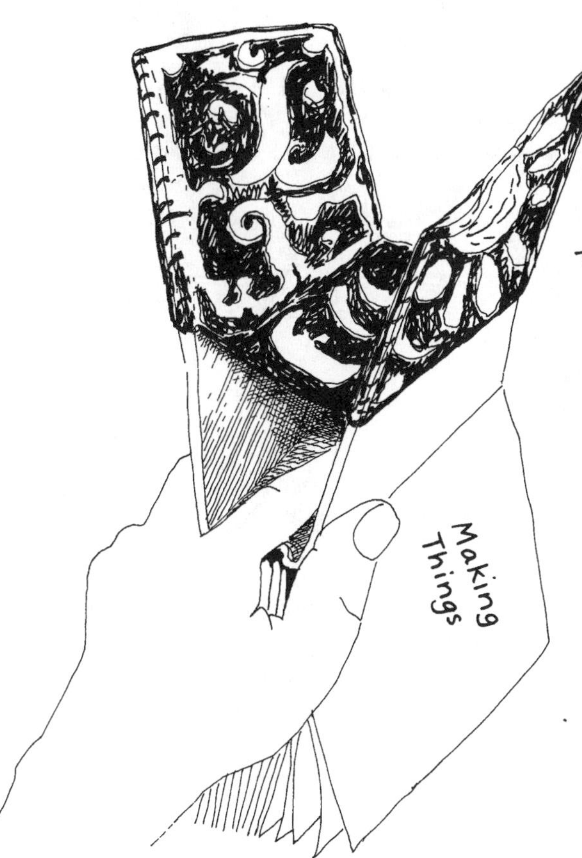

These cloth jackets slip on and off easily and can be washed. They make nice gifts for book lovers.

Make a cover for this book.

BUTTERFLY BOOK

YOU WILL NEED: CARDBOARD • CRAYONS OR MARKERS • SCISSORS • 5 OR MORE SHEETS OF PAPER • PENCIL • NEEDLE AND THREAD

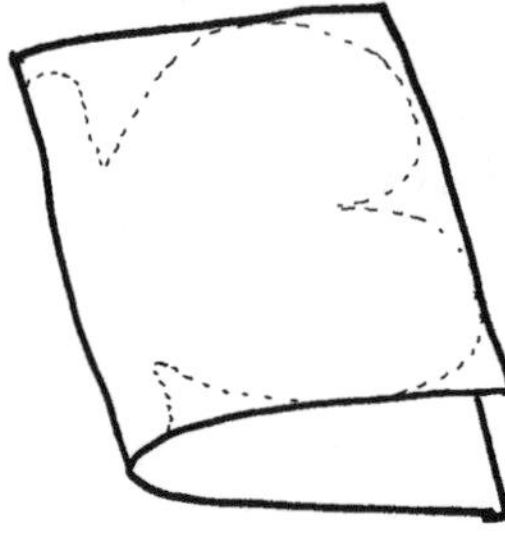

1. Fold cardboard in half. Draw half of a butterfly.

2. Cut out butterfly, and decorate both front and back.

3. Fold stacked set of papers in half. Slip stack into butterfly cover. Trace the butterfly.

4. Cut traced line on stacked pages all at once so they are flush with cover.

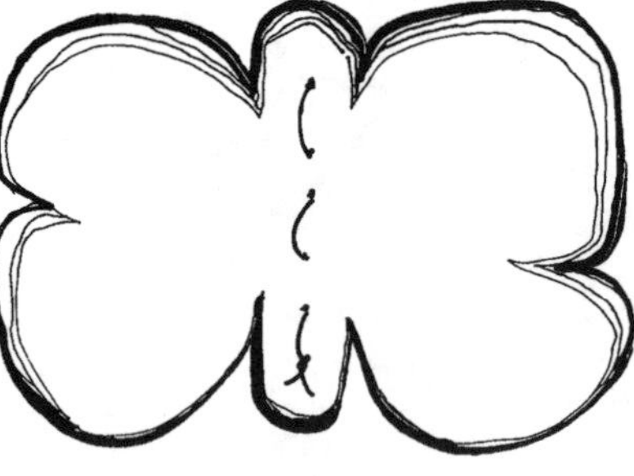

5. Open book out flat, and sew a few stitches along the middle. Or use staples or 2 brass fasteners to hold pages and cover together.

BERNY HOLSCLAW'S

CITY BOOK

AN EGYPTIAN AND CHINESE ACCORDION-STYLE BOOK

YOU WILL NEED:

PAPER • GLUE • CARDBOARD • SCISSORS • CRAYONS OR MARKERS • PENCIL

1. Glue a dozen or so sheets of paper together.
2. Fold them evenly like an accordion.
3. Cut 2 pieces of cardboard the same size as the top of your accordion paper pack.
4. On one piece of cardboard, draw a cityscape or a village street of houses.
5. Cut out both cardboard pieces along the rooftops.
6. Trace the cardboard rooftops onto the paper pack, and cut the paper pages to fit the cardboard covers.
7. Glue first page to front cardboard and last page to back cardboard.
8. Write a tour guide of your town or city.

CLAY LEAVES

YOU WILL NEED:

DRYING CLAY • NAIL • KNIFE • GLAZES (OPTIONAL) • CORD

LEAF BEADS

1. Roll clay into sausage shape.
2. Draw a leaf on flat end with nail point.
3. Cut away excess clay.
4. Slice leaves off loaf. Decorate with nail point.
5. Poke holes while clay is still wet.
6. Let beads dry. String them as is, or glaze and bake them first.

LEAF PENDANT

YOU WILL NEED:

DRYING CLAY
ROLLING PIN
LEAVES
KNIFE
NAIL OR KNITTING NEEDLE
PAINT OR GLAZE (OPTIONAL)
CORD

1. Flatten a ball of clay with rolling pin.
2. Lay a leaf on the clay, and roll over it.
3. Remove leaf. Poke 2 small string holes in clay while it is still wet.
4. When clay is dry, paint it and wear it as a pendant.

PASTA BEADS & PAPER CLIPS

PASTA NECKLACES

YOU WILL NEED:

ANY SHAPE DRIED PASTA WITH HOLES
• BEADS AND BUTTONS • STRING

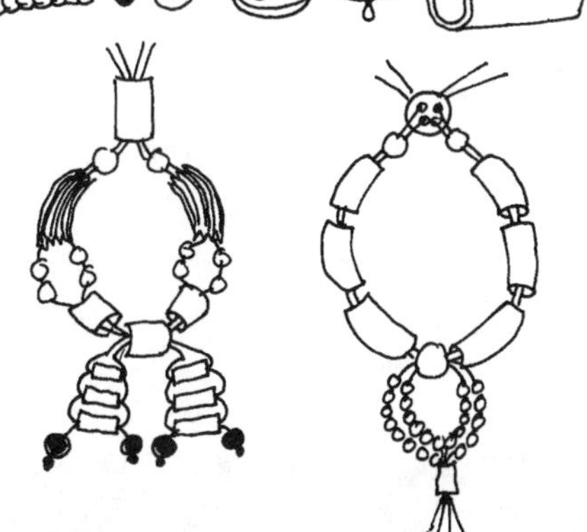

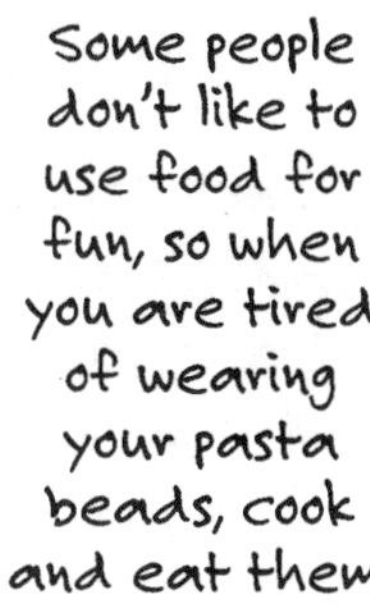

Some people don't like to use food for fun, so when you are tired of wearing your pasta beads, cook and eat them!

PAPER CLIP NECKLACES

I remember the old hair-catching paper clip necklaces we made as kids — this is an improvement, with colored tape wrapped around the open ends. Wear it, or hang it around the Christmas tree.

FINGER PAINTING

YOU WILL NEED:

- PACKET OF CHOCOLATE PUDDING OR OTHER HOMEMADE FINGER PAINTS (SEE RECIPES BELOW)
- COOKIE SHEET
- SLIPPERY SHELF PAPER
- WHITE BOND PAPER

QUICK & EASY CHOCOLATE PUDDING FINGER PAINT

1. Mix as directed on package, a little on the gushy side.
2. Spread pudding on cookie sheet, and just mess about, pressing fingers down to make designs.

   If you want to keep your design, lay a sheet of paper over it (with clean hands!) and press very lightly over the surface. Pull print up slowly. Allow to dry. Make a new design in the pudding.

   OR make your designs directly on sheets of shelf paper. Let them dry.

QUICK COOKED FINGER PAINT

CORNSTARCH RECIPE

1 CUP CORNSTARCH, DILUTED
1 QUART BOILING WATER
$\frac{1}{2}$ CUP SOAP FLAKES

FLOUR RECIPE

USE EGGBEATER TO WHIP
$\frac{1}{4}$ CUP FLOUR INTO 1 CUP WARM WATER.
ADD POWDERED COLOR OR FOOD COLORING.

CRAYON Activities

CRAYON RUBBINGS

1. Peel paper off crayon. Break crayon in two.
2. Choose an object with a raised or textured surface.
3. Place a thin sheet of paper over the object, and draw the broad side of the crayon over the surface.

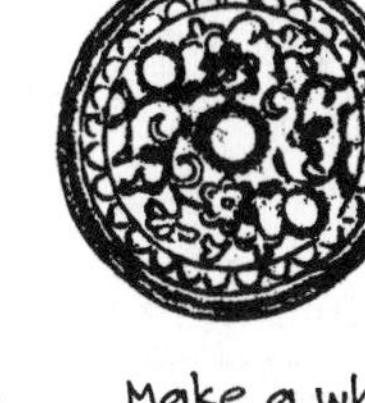

Make a white crayon rubbing, and paint over it with india ink or ebony stain.

Try: coins, fossils, dishes with raised patterns, manhole covers, tombstones, brass bas-reliefs, shells, dry scaly fish, keys, and hundreds of other objects.

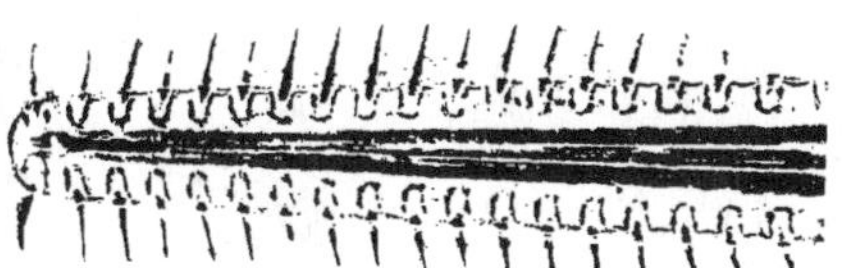

CRAYON "STAINED GLASS"

or oiled paper transparencies

1. Draw a picture using black india ink.
2. Color your design with crayons.
3. Turn picture over. Dab a rag in vegetable oil, and rub oil all over back of picture to make it transparent.
4. Paper towel off the excess oil.
5. Tape your "stained glass" onto a sunny window so the light shines through.

CRAYON SCRATCHBOARDS

1. Cover heavy paper with solid crayon colors in a patchwork design.
2. Over these colors, paint solid black india ink. Let dry.
   OR mix 1 part black poster paint with 4 parts detergent to cover the colors (and make it stick). Let dry.
3. Use a nail, paper clip, or ballpoint pen to scratch a design through the black layer and expose the colors.

Crayons are wonderful for drawing and coloring. The best way to use them is to peel off the paper part and break the crayon into two pieces. (They will break anyway, so you may as well have the fun of doing it on purpose!) Use them every which-way.

MARIONETTES

YOU WILL NEED:

CARDBOARD
CRAYONS OR MARKERS
SCISSORS
BRASS FASTENERS
STRING
STICK OR PENCIL

1. Create your own marionette characters. Draw each body part separately and big enough for fasteners to fit through the holes.
2. Cut out and decorate body parts.
3. Poke or punch holes.
4. Fasten all parts together. (If holes are big, the parts will swing. If holes are tight, the parts will stay stiff. Experiment.)

5. Tie strings to arms and legs. Tie the other ends to stick or pencil. Rock stick or pencil back and forth to make your figure move or dance.

SLOTTED ANIMALS

No nails
Collapsible
Interchangeable

YOU WILL NEED:

CARDBOARD OR STYROFOAM
SCISSORS
CRAYONS OR MARKERS
STRING OR YARN

1. Cut animal parts out, and decorate.
2. Cut slots as shown. Slots should be no wider than cardboard or Styrofoam, or figures will wobble.

Then make big ones, to climb on, out of wood.

Design a cat, a horse . . . or is it a cow?

CLIMBING PULL TOYS

YOU WILL NEED:

6" x 8" x 1" PIECE OF WOOD • FELT-TIP MARKERS • COPING SAW • DRILL • 7" x 1" WOODEN STICK FOR HOLDING BAR • STRING • 2 BEADS OR BUTTONS • CUP HOOK

1. On piece of wood, draw a figure, with arms outstretched.
2. Cut out figure with a coping saw.
3. Drill holes vertically through its hands.
4. Drill 3 holes in holding bar: a center hole and one at each end, big enough for string.
5. Cut two 5' pieces of string.
6. Thread strings through holding bar at each side, and secure with a knot or bead.
7. Thread strings through hand holes of figure. Tie a bead or button at end of strings.

HOLDING BAR

←6"→

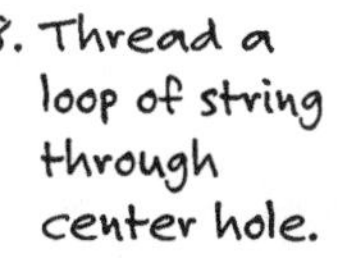

8. Thread a loop of string through center hole.
9. Screw cup hook into doorway. Attach holding bar to hook.
0. Pull strings, alternating left and right, to make your figure climb up the strings.
1. Relax tension to make figure slide down again.

TIN LID ORNAMENTS

YOU WILL NEED:

- TIN-CAN LID
- WOOD BLOCK FOR POUNDING SURFACE
- NAIL
- HAMMER
- SCISSORS OR TIN SNIPS
- THREAD

1. Put flat lid on pounding surface. Hammer round holes with nail point and long holes with side of nail head.
2. Bend lid around hammer handle.
3. Hang by thread.

Cut on red lines.

HAMMERED WIRE JEWELRY

YOU WILL NEED:

THIN AND HEAVY BRASS AND COPPER WIRE • THIN-NOSED PLIERS • WIRE CUTTERS • DOWEL • HAMMER • METAL POUNDING SURFACE • EARRING BACKS

Bend wire around dowel for links and curls. Hammer on steel or iron pounding surface to flatten wire curls. Cut with wire cutters.

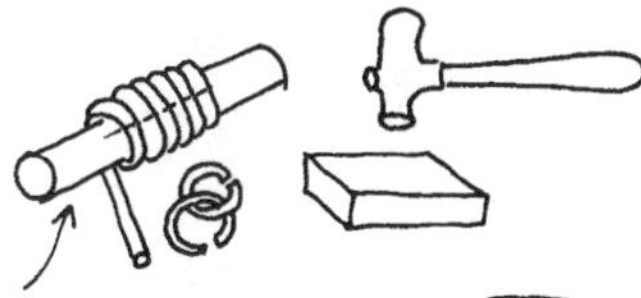

To make a wire bending jig, place nails or dowel pegs in a block of wood.

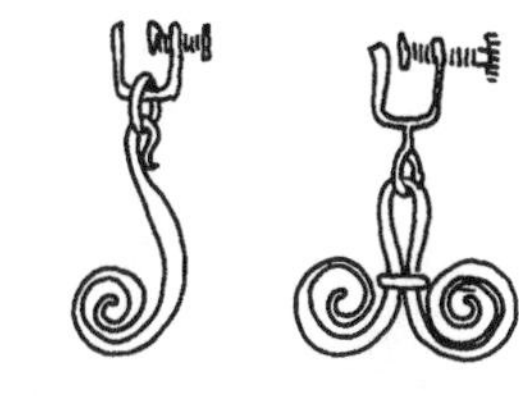

CATCH PIN

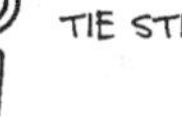

TIE STICK

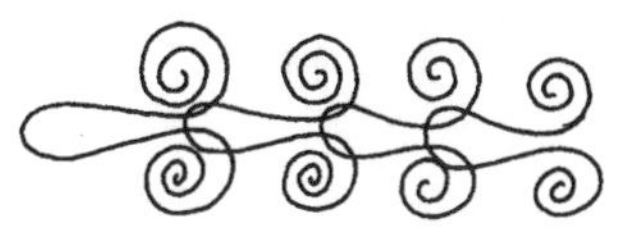

HAMMERED LINKED CURLS

CLASP DESIGNS

BALANCING TOYS

MILK CARTON BALANCER

YOU WILL NEED:

MILK CARTON • 2 THIN STICKS • 2 BALLS OF PLASTICINE • PENCIL

Build balancer as shown, and poise it on a taut string. Make adjustments if needed.

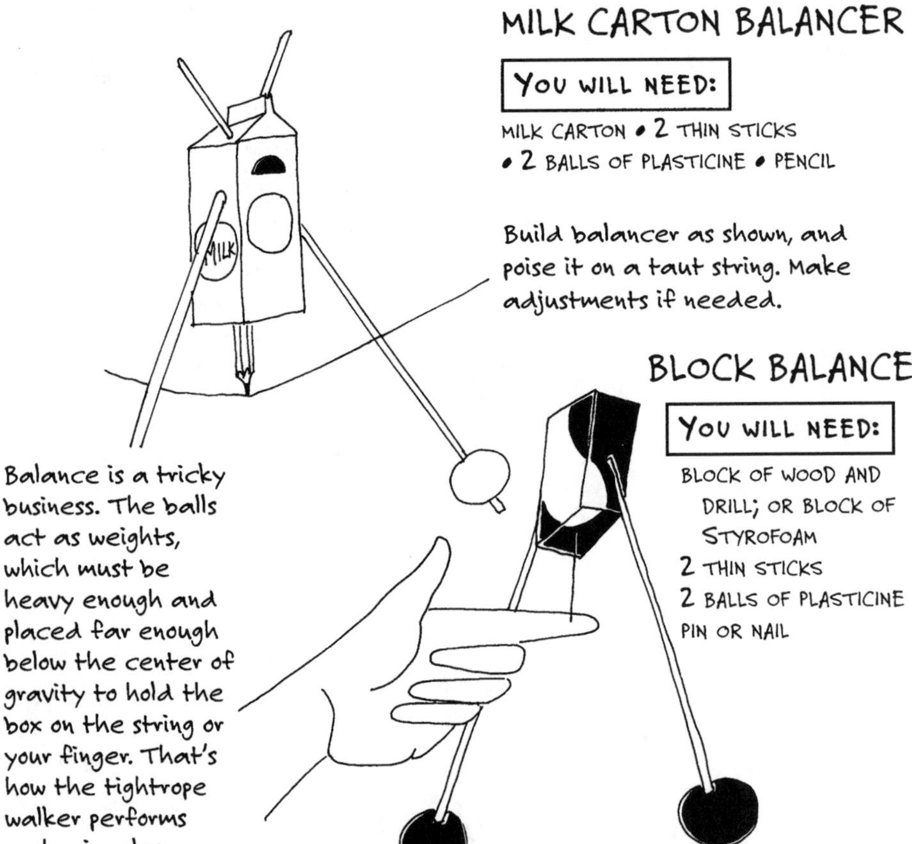

BLOCK BALANCER

YOU WILL NEED:

BLOCK OF WOOD AND DRILL; OR BLOCK OF STYROFOAM
2 THIN STICKS
2 BALLS OF PLASTICINE
PIN OR NAIL

Balance is a tricky business. The balls act as weights, which must be heavy enough and placed far enough below the center of gravity to hold the box on the string or your finger. That's how the tightrope walker performs such miracles.

1. Drill 2 holes in block of wood at an angle to hold sticks OR poke sticks into block of Styrofoam (glue them if they're loose). Note the angle of the balancing arms; it's important — not too wide and not too steep.
2. Center the pivotal pin or nail.
3. Attach clay balls to ends of sticks, heavy enough to act as weights. Squeeze them tight so they won't fall off. The block should balance so well on your finger that you could run without it falling off.

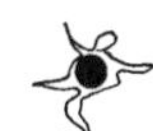

FEATHER BALANCER

YOU WILL NEED:

FEATHER
2 PAPER CLIPS
PLASTICINE BALL
PLASTICINE STAND

1. Straighten paper clips.
2. Bend a loop in the center of one clip. Stick one end into feather stem, the other end into plasticine ball.
3. Bend clip 2 into an arch as shown. Make a hook in one end. Stick the other end into plasticine stand. Attach loop to hook so feather balances freely. It should balance if weight is right.

PRUNE-AND-CORK BALANCER

YOU WILL NEED:

CORK (NOT TOO BIG)
2 HEAVY PRUNES
2 PAPER CLIPS
PIN
PENCIL WITH ERASER

1. Straighten paper clips.
2. Poke them through cork above center.
3. Hook prunes on each end. (For more weight, add more prunes.)
4. Poke pin into pencil eraser. Balance cork on pin. Adjust as needed.

Little and heavy things balance big and light things.

MOBILES

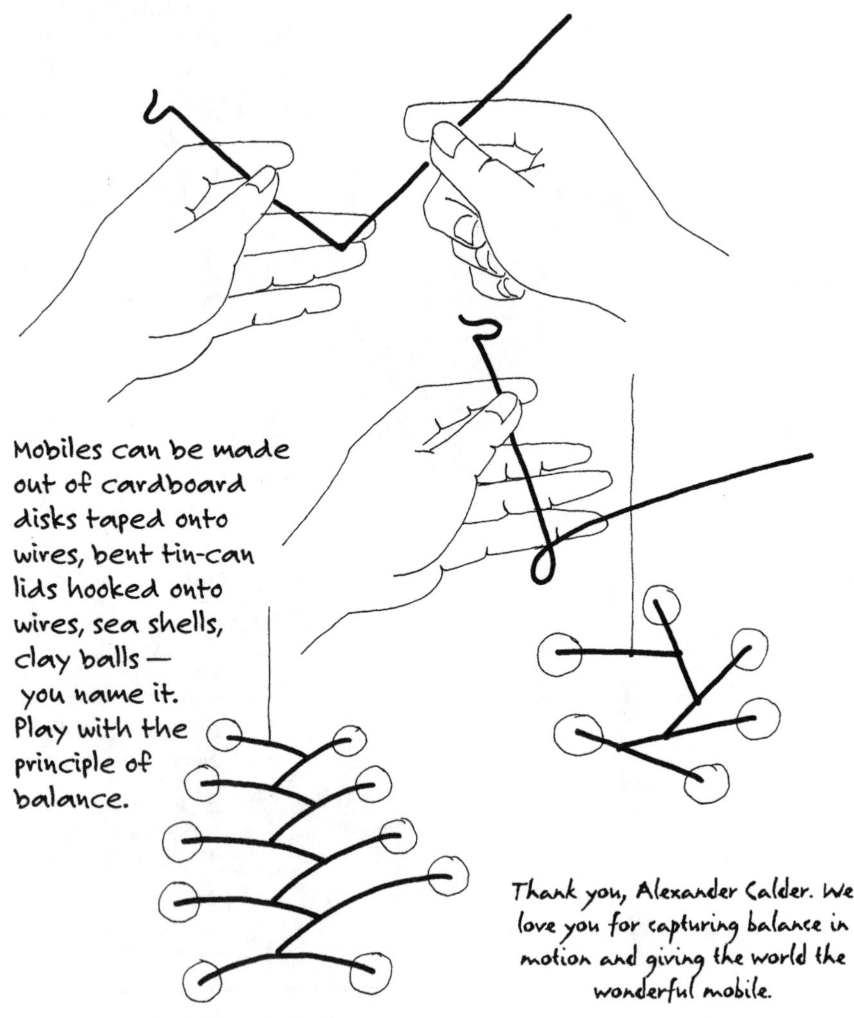

Mobiles can be made out of cardboard disks taped onto wires, bent tin-can lids hooked onto wires, sea shells, clay balls — you name it. Play with the principle of balance.

Thank you, Alexander Calder. We love you for capturing balance in motion and giving the world the wonderful mobile.

BALANCING SHAPES

BALANCING MOON OR BALANCING BIRD

YOU WILL NEED:

HEAVY CARDBOARD AND SCISSORS; OR WOOD, SAW, AND DRILL
CRAYONS OR MARKERS
PAPER CLIP
KEYS, NUTS, AND LEAD WEIGHTS

1. Draw the half-moon shape shown below.
2. Cut shape out.
3. Make a hole for weight hook at bottom.
4. Bend paper clip into hook shape, and attach it.
5. Put weights on hook until you achieve balance.

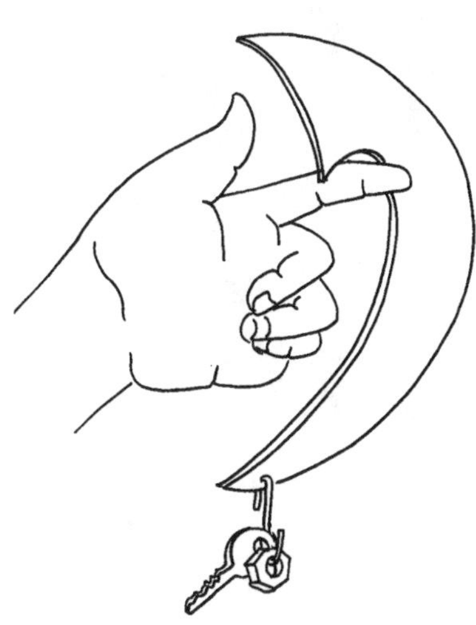

Try it with this shape. Make the tail long enough to ensure balance below center of gravity.

See how many nuts, keys, or lead weights it takes to balance this bird on your finger.

See what else you can make out of this basic half-moon shape.

STRAW MOBILE
Turn the book this way — try for horizontal balance!
YOU WILL NEED:
PLASTIC STRAWS
SCISSORS
NEEDLE AND THREAD
AND A STEADY FINGER TO
CHECK AND CORRECT BALAN
(AS SHOWN IN
THE DRAWING ABOVE)
ETC.
#5
#4
#3

lace straws on these pages, and cut them to size.

2. Thread the needle, and tie a knot in the end of the thread. Poke needle through the center of straw #1 (shown at the <u>bottom</u> of this page).

3. Poke needle through straw #2, about an inch in from one end. Cut thread, and tie a knot, allowing for about $1\frac{1}{2}$" between straws.

4. Balance straw #2 on your finger to find the center of balance.

5. Attach straw #3 at that balancing point.

6. Continue adding as many straws as you like. Then hang your mobile up in a drafty place.

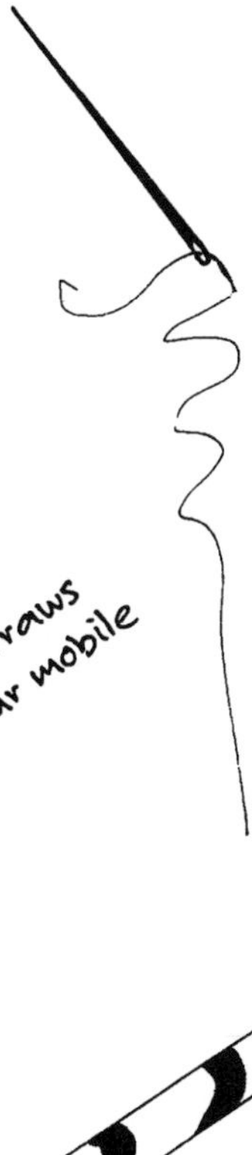

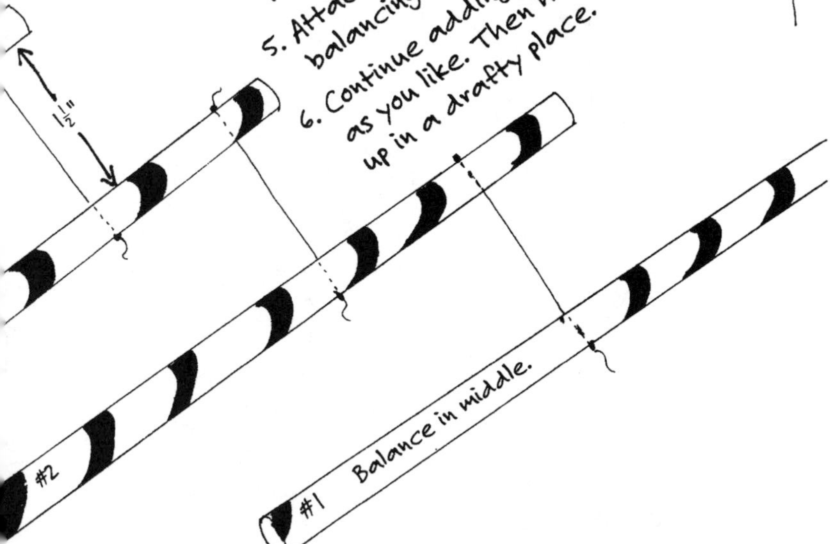

1½"

#2

#1 Balance in middle.

SALT PENDULUM

YOU WILL NEED:

SMALL FUNNEL OR CONE OF HEAVY PAPER, TAPED CLOSED WITH CUT NOSE • TABLE SALT • STRING • BLACK PAPER • 2 CUP HOOKS

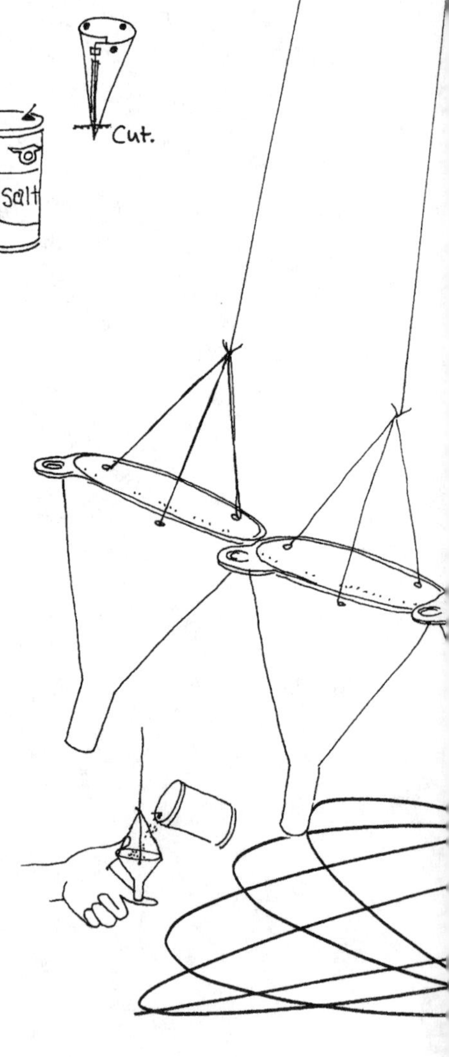

1. Poke 3 equidistant holes in top rim of funnel.
2. Attach 3 equal-length strings (about 4") to holes, and knot together at top.
3. Put cup hooks in either side of a doorway.

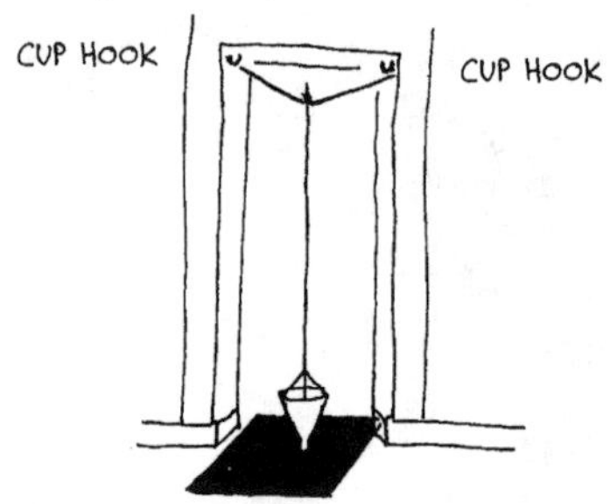

4. Tie cross string from one hook to the other.
5. Tie another string to center of cross string, long enough to hold funnel just off the floor. Tie other end of string to funnel strings.
6. Place black paper on floor across doorway.
7. Fill funnel with salt, holding it with your finger to plug hole.

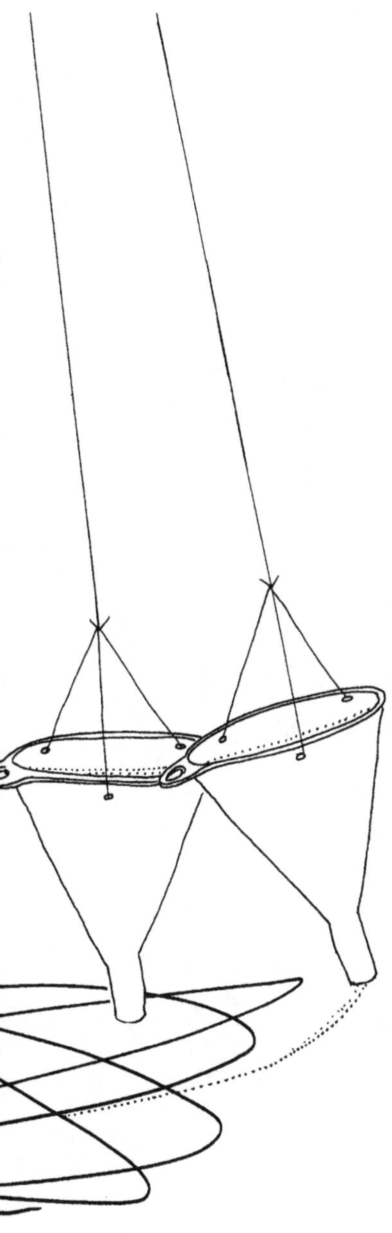

8. Let go as you start pendulum gently swinging.
9. Watch the pendulum draw beautiful geometric designs.

Note: You can also use sifted sand with uniform particles. It must be dry to flow nicely. Hole of funnel must be in proportion to size of particles. Experiment until you have a good flow.

You can make little and giant pendulums. At the Children's Museum, we built a 30' sand pendulum and let visiting children swing the pendulum and sweep up the designs. The Boston Science Museum has an even bigger one-point harness Foucault pendulum that proves the earth's rotation.

BED FRIENDS & UMMM-DEARS

YOU WILL NEED:

SOFT OLD UNDERSHIRT OR COTTON FABRIC • INDELIBLE PEN OR FELT-TIP MARKER • SCISSORS • NEEDLE AND THREAD • OLD STOCKINGS OR PILLOW STUFFING

1. Draw a friend on the undershirt or muslin.
2. Cut it out double.

3. Turn doll inside out, and sew 2 sides together, leaving about 3" open on one side.
4. Turn doll right side out. Stuff and sew closed.

PILLOW COZIES

YOU WILL NEED:

PILLOWCASE
INDELIBLE MARKER
NEWSPAPER
PAPER TOWEL
IRON

1. Use indelible marker to outline a big cozy animal on your pillowcase. Fill in colors with crayons, pressing hard.
2. Put a thick pack of newspaper inside pillowcase and one sheet of paper towel on top of your drawing.
3. Iron it until all the wax melts out into the paper towel, leaving the drawing permanently printed on the pillowcase. Wash gently in warm water.

You can make 4 cozies and change them every week.

MOUSE POUCH

YOU WILL NEED:

A PAIR OF GLASSES • FELT • SCISSORS • GLUE • NEEDLE AND THREAD • YARN (OPTIONAL) • SNAP OR VELCRO; OR RIBBON

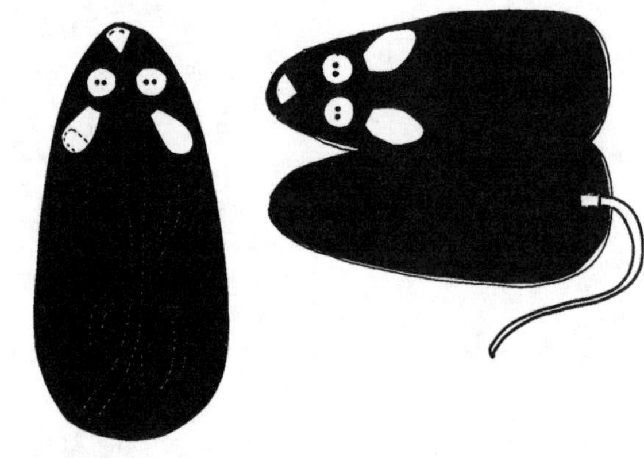

1. Place the glasses on 2 pieces of felt, and trace around them in the shape of a mouse, as shown here.
2. Cut tracing out double, allowing about $\frac{1}{2}$" margin.
3. Make eyes, ears, and nose shapes any way you like. Sew or glue them on. Attach some kind of a tail.
4. Sew edges together from ear to ear, leaving mouth open big enough to slide glasses in and out.
5. Sew snap or Velcro inside mouth. Or attach a ribbon, and wear the pouch around your neck.

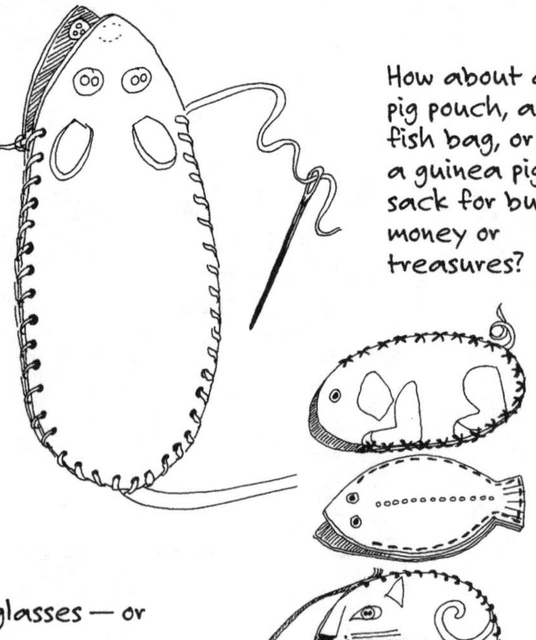

How about a pig pouch, a fish bag, or a guinea pig sack for bus money or treasures?

Good for holding Granny's glasses — or whatever you like

APPLIQUÉ & STITCHERY

1. Cut out simple designs of one color, and sew them onto another color, turning the edges under as you go.

YOU WILL NEED:

COTTON SCRAPS
SCISSORS
NEEDLE AND THREAD
EMBROIDERY THREAD

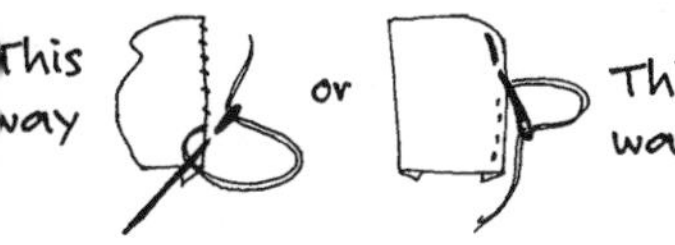

2. Stitch in details with embroidery thread.

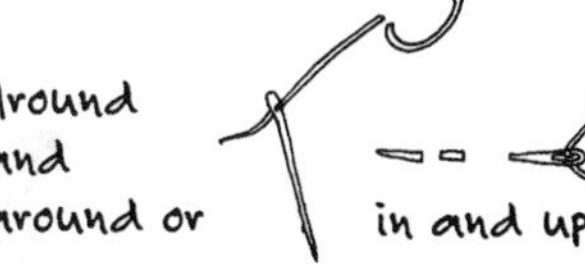

SAN BLAS CUT-AWAY APPLIQUÉ

1. Cut 3 rectangles of red, yellow, and black cotton fabric — or any 3 colors you like (about 9" x 12" works well). Put black on top, then red, then yellow.
2. Sew the 3 layers together loosely at edges to hold them.
3. Draw with pencil or chalk on black layer.
4. Cut through black to expose red layer. Turn cut edges under, and sew them down.
5. Cut details through red layer to expose yellow layer, leaving fat red margins. Turn edges under, and sew.

The San Blas Islanders make a real art of this, called molas.

STITCHES

Read the pictures and try — easy as pie. . . .

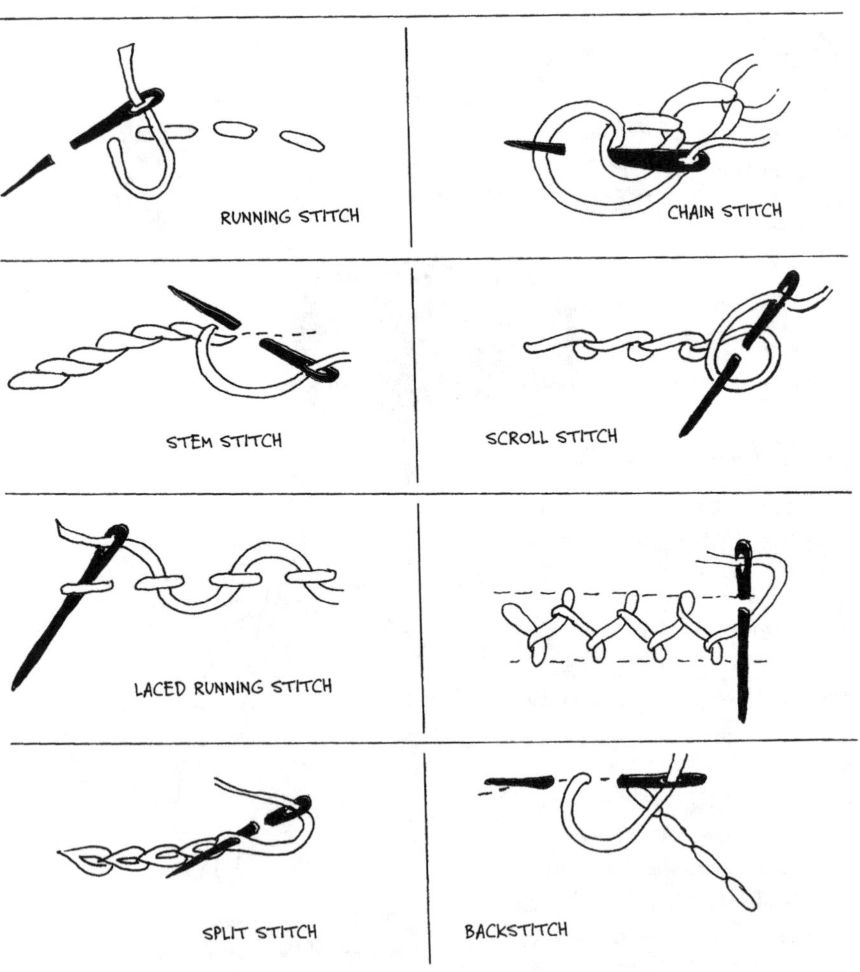

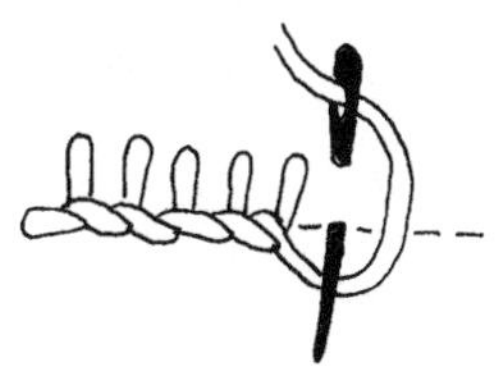

BLANKET STITCH

FERN STITCH

FISH BONE

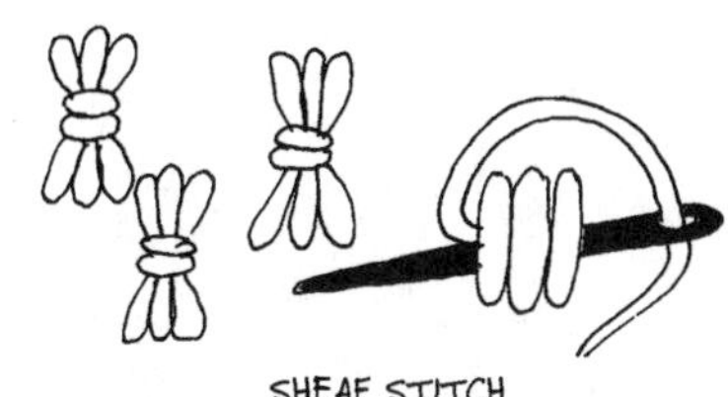

SHEAF STITCH

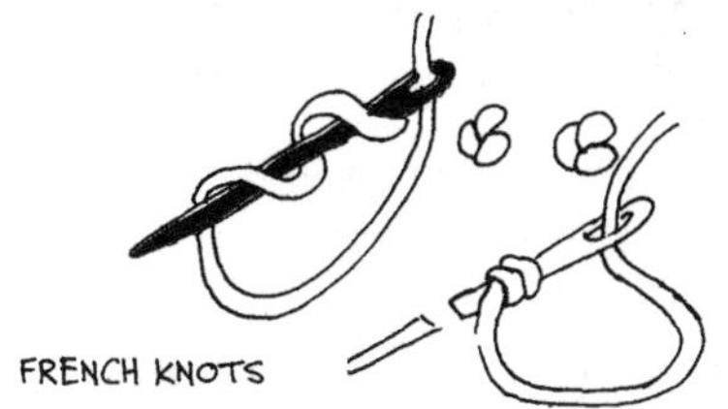

FRENCH KNOTS

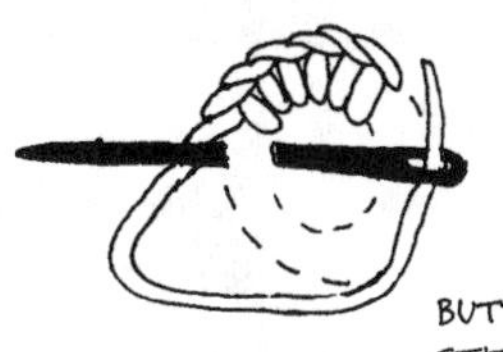

BUTTONHOLE STITCH

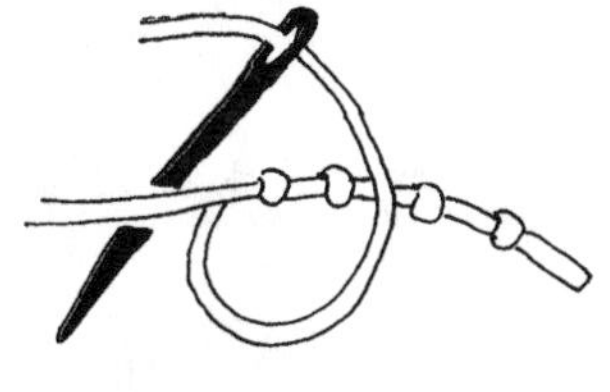

HERRINGBONE STITCH

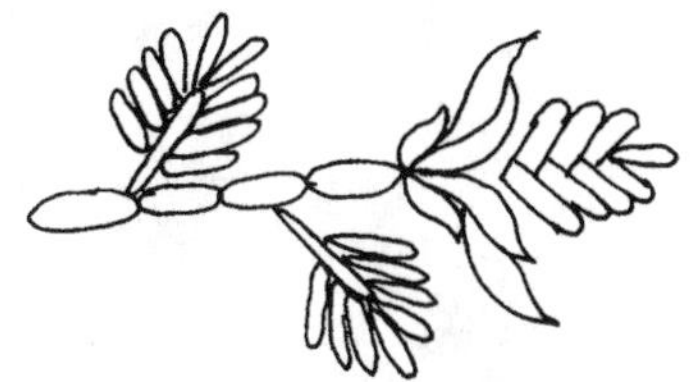

RUG HOOKING

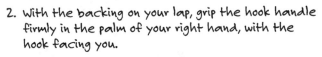

YOU WILL NEED:

BURLAP OR COTTON MONK'S CLOTH • BLACK MARKER • RUG HOOK • HEAVY YARN OR STRIPS OF FABRIC

1. Draw a simple design directly on the burlap or cotton backing material.

2. With the backing on your lap, grip the hook handle firmly in the palm of your right hand, with the hook facing you.

3. With your left hand, prepare a loop at one end of your yarn, and hold it on the underside of the backing. Poke the hook through the backing, catch the loop, and pull it through to the front. (Wiggle the mesh open and twist your wrist to avoid catching the threads of the backing on the hook.) Pull the loop all the way through so the tail stands about 1" high.

4. Prepare the next loop with your left hand, and pull it through so it stands about $\frac{1}{2}$" high. Make loops quite close together in a row.

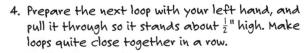

5. Continue in this manner, making all the loops the same height. (Twist your wrist away from you to avoid pulling out the previous stitch.)

The left hand has a double job: It must hold the backing on your lap and feed the yarn to the hook every time it appears on the underside.

It will help to clamp the yarn between the first two fingers of your left hand so it won't twist or fold and you'll have tension to pull against.

6. When you come to the end of the yarn or strip, pull the tail end up as you did with the first stitch, and cut both tails even with the loops.

7. Continue your loops all the way around the margin line, turning your backing as you go so you can work toward yourself. To square the corners, clip the corner loop.

8. If you want to start a new color, clip the old yarn, pull the tail up, and start the new yarn in the same hole.

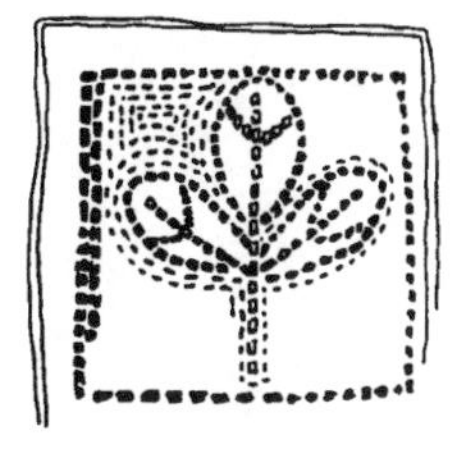

9. The next row of loops should sit about two weave threads away from the first row. Don't crowd. Don't jump around. Keep hooking close to the last loop. Keep the back flat and tidy.

Fill in areas of your design by hooking:

in a zigzag

back and forth

in circles

in squares

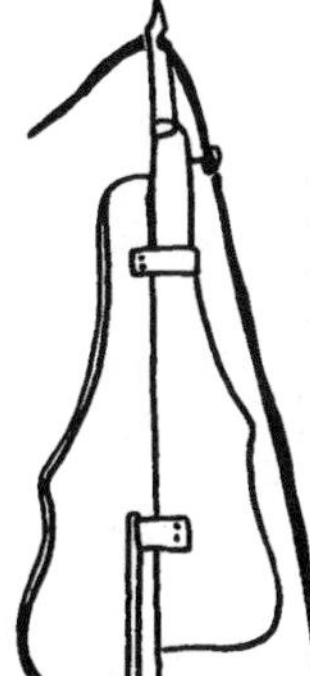

SHUTTLE HOOK (FOR SPEEDIER HOOKING)
TURN TO PAGE 152 TO SEE TWO LARGE TAPESTRIES THAT WERE MADE USING SHUTTLE HOOKS.

STRAIGHT RUG HOOK

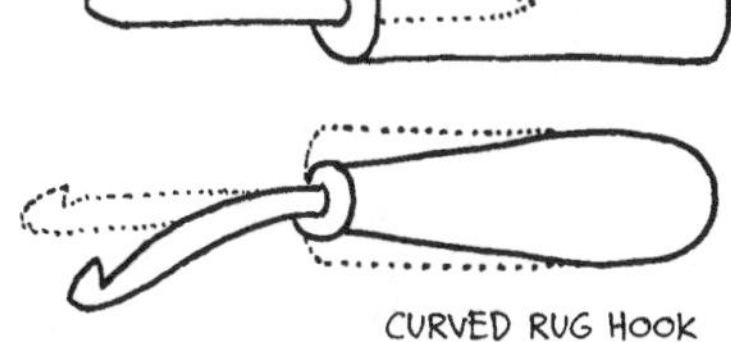

CURVED RUG HOOK

You can make your own hook out of a nail and a dowel.

PORTABLE HOUSES

Once you've made a cardboard model, try making one from wood.

YOU WILL NEED:

CORRUGATED CARDBOARD BOX
RULER
MAT KNIFE
2 DOWELS (SAME WIDTH AS ROOF)
MARKERS

CARDBOARD HOUSE

1. Cut roof and floor in one piece, with roof slots as shown. Score and bend.
2. Cut out front and back.

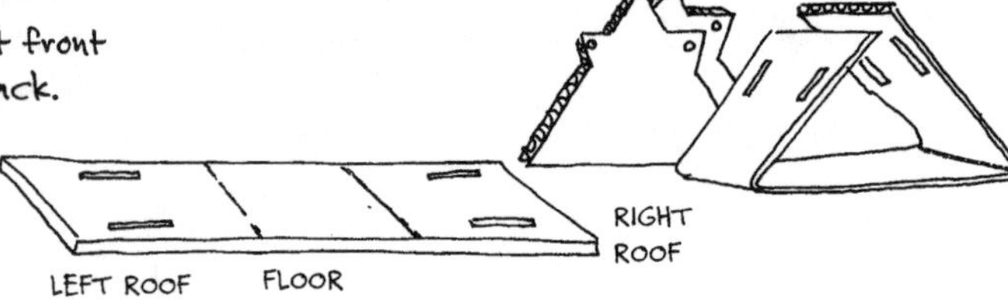

3. Fit them into roof slots and mark dowel holes. Holes must be close to roof.
4. Poke holes so dowels will fit tight. Slide them through. Decorate.

YOU WILL NEED:

PLYWOOD • 2 DOWELS (SAME WIDTH AS ROOF) • SAW • DRILL

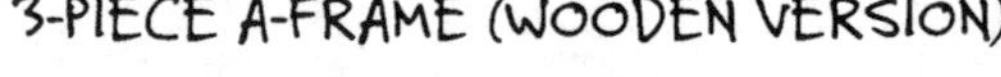

3-PIECE A-FRAME (WOODEN VERSION)

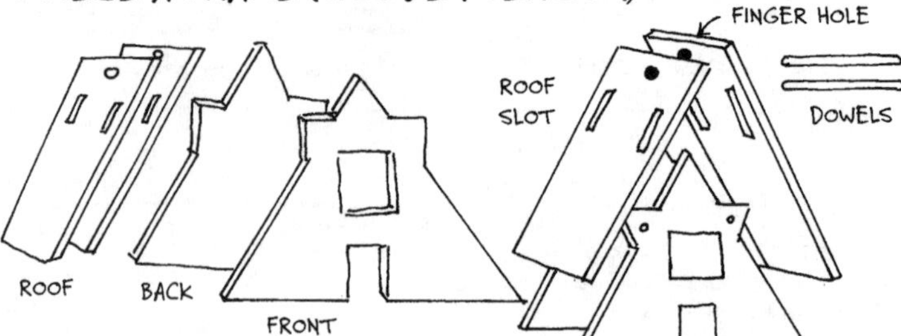

1. Cut, decorate, and assemble these 4 pieces.
2. Make dowel holes close to roof board. Roof slots and dowel holes are the key!

BOX HOUSES

YOU WILL NEED:

BIG OR SMALL CORRUGATED CARDBOARD BOX

- SCISSORS
- TAPE
- CRAYONS OR MARKERS

1. Cut box along dotted lines shown here.
2. Cut hand holes.
3. Score and bend inward to make roof.

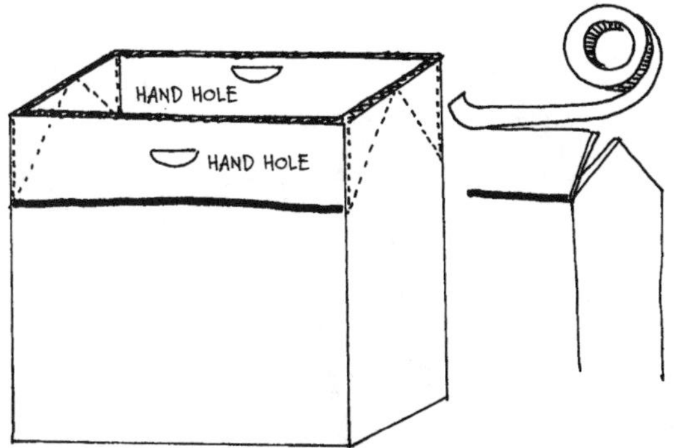

4. Tape roof together OR tie hand holes together in case you want to rearrange the inside now and then.
5. Decorate.

You can make a house to sit in if you can get a refrigerator box.

From quiet homes and first beginnings
Out to the undiscovered ends,
There's nothing worth the price of winning,
But laughter and the love of friends.

— Hilaire Belloc

BOX HORSE

YOU WILL NEED:

WOODEN BOX • PINE BOARD • SAW • HAMMER AND NAILS • ROPE OR STRING • DRILL • 4 FURNITURE CASTERS • SIXTEEN $\frac{3}{4}$" SCREWS • SCREWDRIVER • MARKERS OR PAINTS

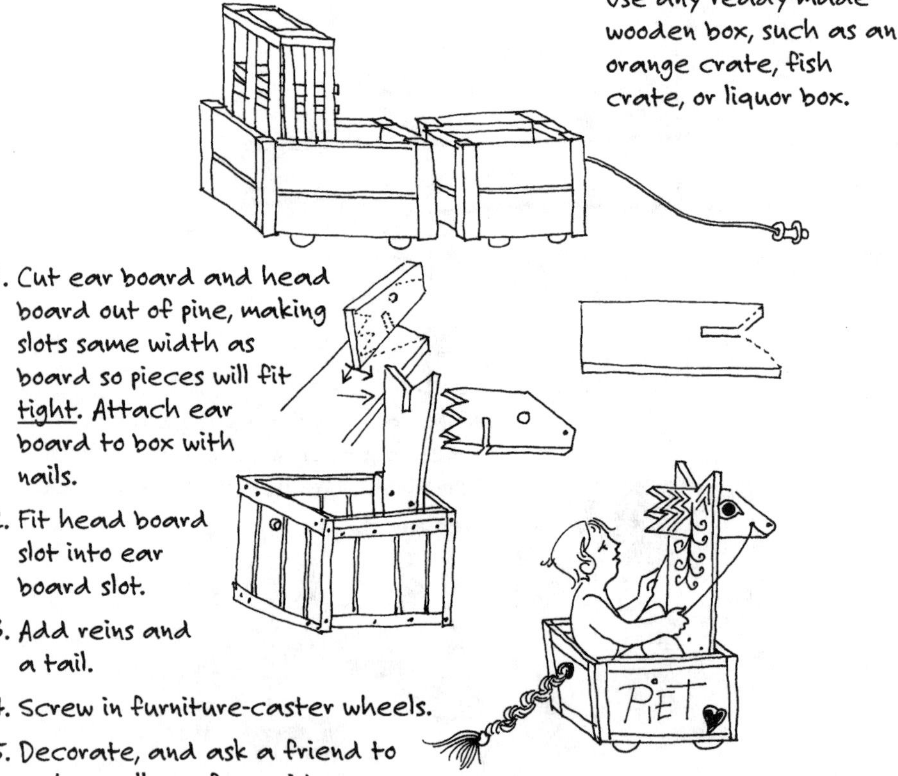

Use any ready-made wooden box, such as an orange crate, fish crate, or liquor box.

1. Cut ear board and head board out of pine, making slots same width as board so pieces will fit tight. Attach ear board to box with nails.
2. Fit head board slot into ear board slot.
3. Add reins and a tail.
4. Screw in furniture-caster wheels.
5. Decorate, and ask a friend to push or pull you for a ride.

Ready-to-screw-on furniture casters, found at hardware stores, make fine wheels.

Make the horse's neck long enough so the child doesn't bump into the horse's mane.

CARDBOARD RACING TURTLES

YOU WILL NEED:

DISH FOR TRACING • CARDBOARD • PENCIL • CRAYONS, MARKERS, OR PAINTS • SCISSORS • STRING

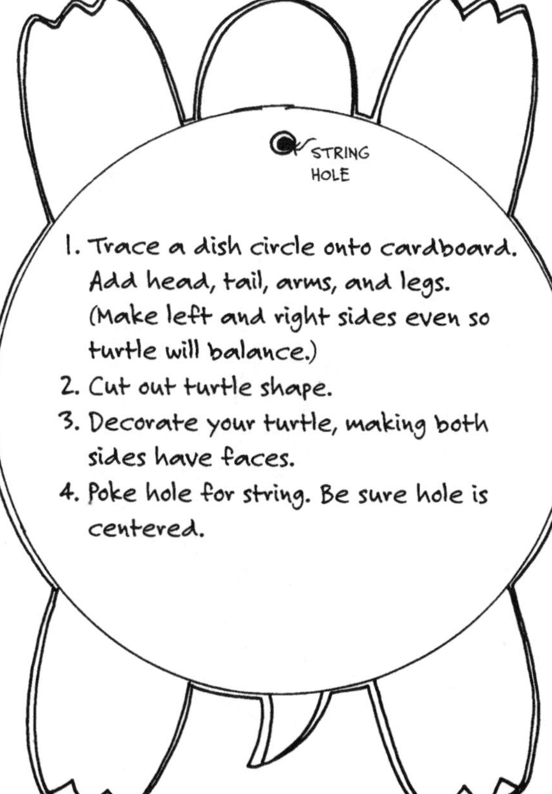

1. Trace a dish circle onto cardboard. Add head, tail, arms, and legs. (Make left and right sides even so turtle will balance.)
2. Cut out turtle shape.
3. Decorate your turtle, making both sides have faces.
4. Poke hole for string. Be sure hole is centered.
5. Cut 10' of string. Tie one end to a table leg 7" up. Thread other end through turtle's string hole.
6. Pull string taut, and turtle will stand; release and it'll flop forward. Pull-flop turtle to top of string, then flip it over and pull-flop it home.

Make 3. Have a race.

My mother introduced this game to us as children, and I've never seen it played anywhere else. Yet it is so simple and such fun, especially when grown-ups join in.

STILTS

YOU WILL NEED:

TWO 2"-DIAMETER POSTS OR 1" x 1 $\frac{1}{2}$" WOOD STRIPS 6' LONG DEPENDING ON HOW BIG YOU ARE • 6" x 4" x 1 $\frac{1}{2}$" WOOD BLOCK • SANDPAPER • SAW • DRILL • 2" OR 2 $\frac{1}{2}$" SCREWS • SCREWDRIVER

Stilts are used
to raise people off flooded ground,
to reach fruits on tall trees,
to see over high fences,
to look like a giant in the circus,
or just to make you feel BIG
and tall.

I'll never forget Sam Warren, who made me my first pair of stilts and raised them from low to high as I gained confidence. He was kind to children. Someone must have been kind to him and he passed it on.

1. Sandpaper the posts smooth.
2. Cut foot-blocks.
3. Decide on height of foot-block from the ground (start low!).
4. Drill foot-block holes.
5. Screw blocks to posts.

4"
6"
$1\frac{1}{2}$"
2 FOOT-BLOCKS

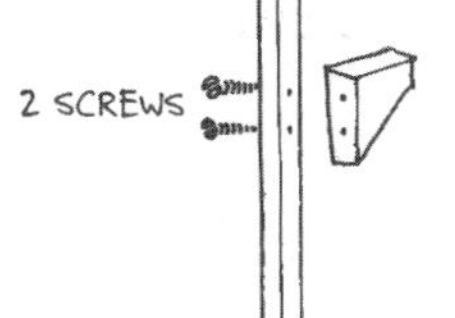

ACTION

a. Stand on a step or box to get started.
b. Put stilt poles under your arms.
c. Climb onto foot-blocks.
d. Walk forward by shifting your weight from one foot to the other, holding the foot-blocks up tightly against your feet.

(If starting and balancing is hard, lean against a wall or ask a friend to hold you until you get the hang of it.)

EASY TIN-CAN FOOT RISERS

Use big tomato cans, bottom ends up. Poke holes for strings. Stand on cans. Hold strings tight, and walk. . . .

THE WIRE HANGER

BIRD FEEDER

Note: The hangers hook onto clothesline in opposite directions and are tied together.

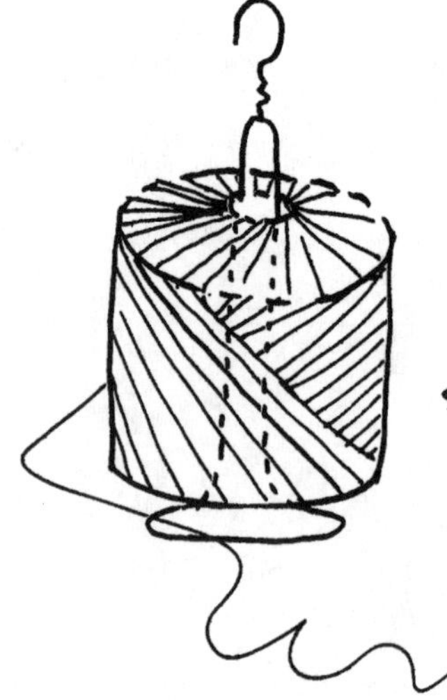

STRING DISPENSER

Bend hanger to hold string.

PANTS HANGER

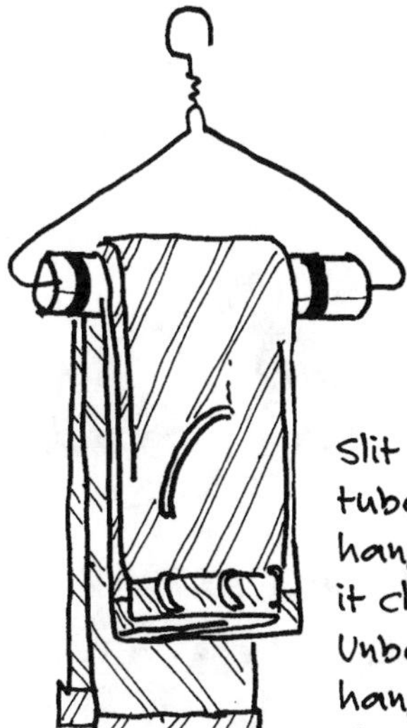

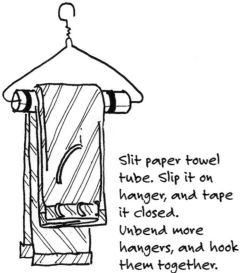

Slit paper towel tube. Slip it on hanger, and tape it closed. Unbend more hangers, and hook them together.

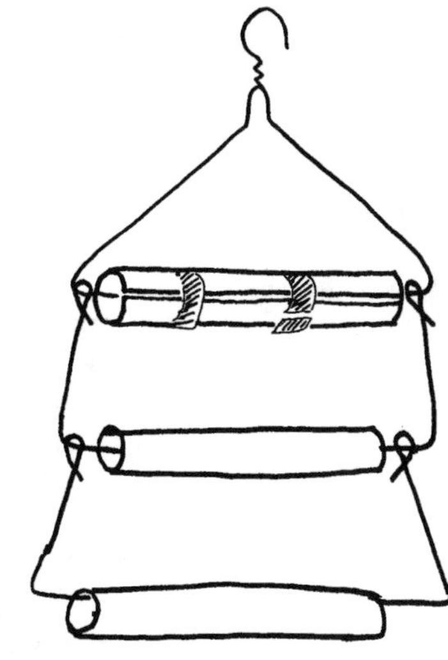

Choose the heaviest wire or wood hanger for strength.

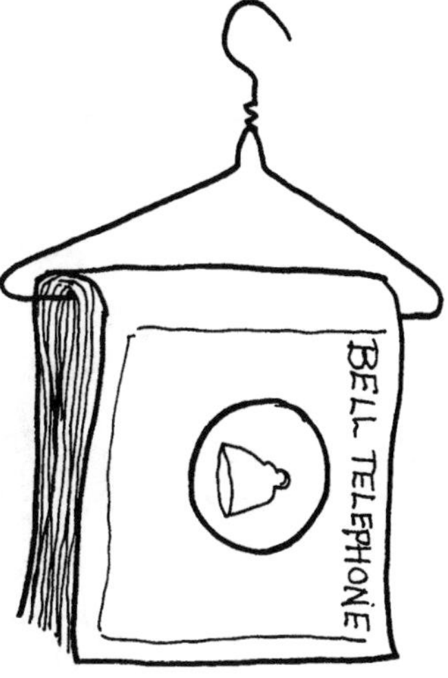

CAMPING AIDS

TRIPOD

Tin-can tripod: no nails, no string, no digging of holes; for boiling water or soup

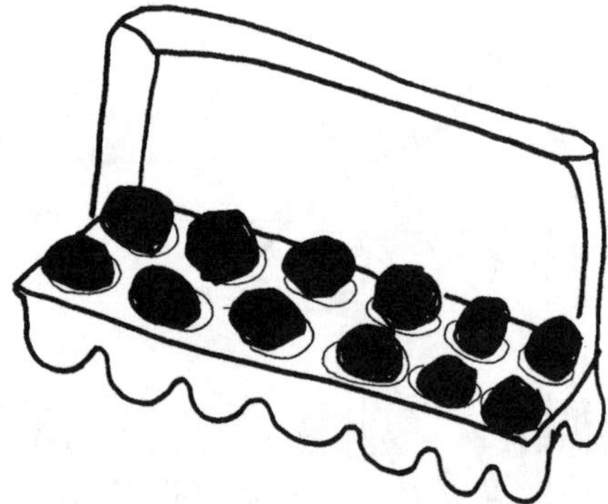

CHARCOAL CARRIER

Fill cardboard egg carton with coal or charcoal. Clean storage. Easy to carry.

SHARPENER

A clay flowerpot makes a pretty good whetstone. Draw blade at an angle along the lip of the pot.

FISH SCALER

Nail bottle cap to flat stick or ruler.
(Put salt on fish board to keep fish from slipping around.)

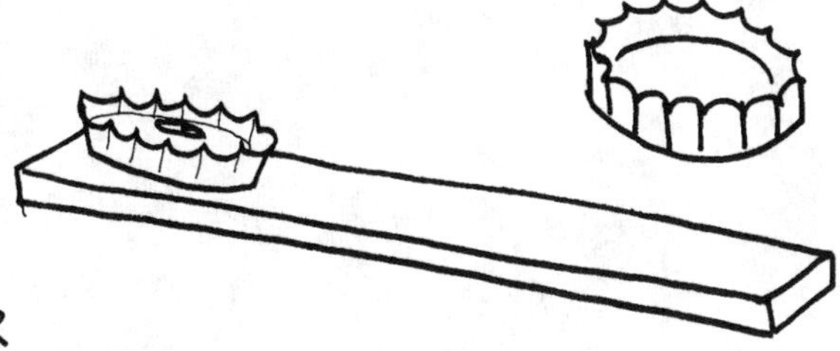

MAP KEEPER

Open can at both ends.

Make a tin-can sleeve for maps and drawings.

FUNNEL OR BAILER

Rinse out a plastic bottle.

Cut bottom off for a funnel.

Cut top off at an angle, and you have a boat bailer.

GRASS HATS, MATS, SACKS, AND SOLES FOR THE FEET

In many traditional cultures, people have turned grasses and weeds bound with sinew, strips of bark, or vines into mats to protect themselves from the damp, cold earth; hats to shield their heads from the sun; containers to carry things in; and hammocks to rock babies in.

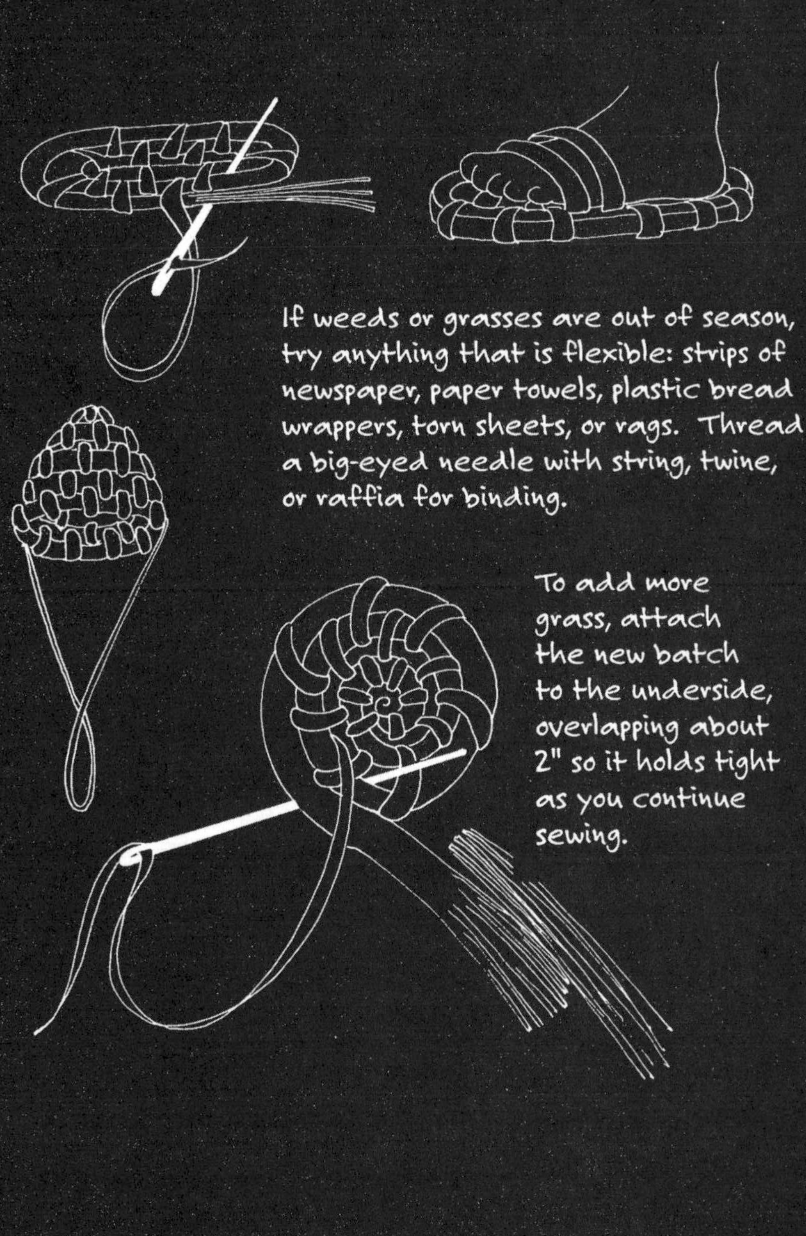

If weeds or grasses are out of season, try anything that is flexible: strips of newspaper, paper towels, plastic bread wrappers, torn sheets, or rags. Thread a big-eyed needle with string, twine, or raffia for binding.

To add more grass, attach the new batch to the underside, overlapping about 2" so it holds tight as you continue sewing.

ANIMATED MOTION

Movies — what a fantastic idea!

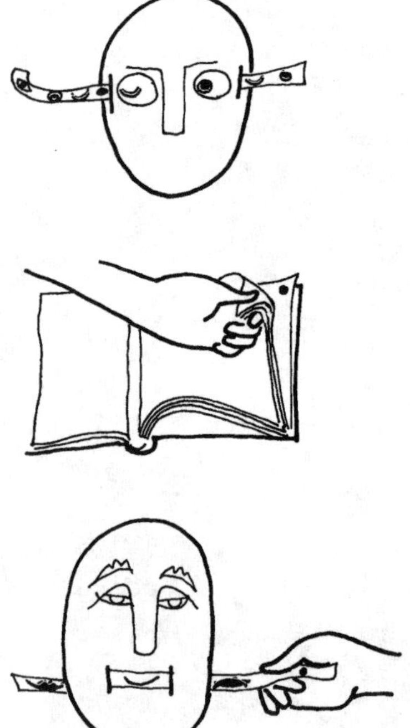

You can pull a filmstrip of eyeballs through a mask and animate a still face. You can open and close a conversation and smile and frown.

Look — I have drawn a figure on the top corner of every right-hand page of this book, so you can see a flip movie by snapping the corners fast.

Experiment with your own flip movies. Try making one figure spin or jump. This may start you on your career as a filmmaker or animation artist!

ZOETROPE

YOU WILL NEED:

CARDBOARD CANISTER (THE KIND ICE CREAM COMES IN) OR MAKE ONE BY ROLLING STIFF CARDBOARD INTO A CYLINDER ABOUT 8–10" IN DIAMETER • MAT KNIFE OR SERRATED KITCHEN KNIFE • SCISSORS • WHITE PAPER • BLACK MARKER • PLASTIC LAZY SUSAN (INEXPENSIVE ONES CAN BE FOUND AT MOST HARDWARE STORES.) • TAPE • FLASHLIGHT OR LIGHTBULB

1. Cut $\frac{3}{4}$" slots halfway down canister, every 2" all the way around, leaving about $\frac{1}{2}$" between slots.
2. Cut 3" strips of paper to fit inside canister.
3. Draw an action sequence such as a stick spinning, ball bouncing, child running, person going up stairs, fish swimming, flower growing, etc.
4. Place movie strip inside canister just below slots, picture side showing.
5. Spin the lazy Susan. Look through the slots, and see the action.

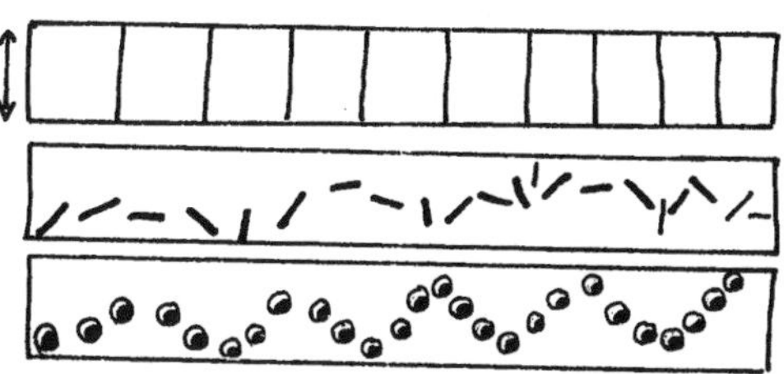

Note:
The movie needs to be well lit. The drawing needs to be good and dark. The inside of the canister can be painted black.

KITES

Kites have always delighted people of all ages.
Kites brought electricity down to earth.
Kites took souls to heaven.
Kites were used for signals during the world wars.
Kites gave people an understanding of air currents, balance, wind changes, gliding, and the ratio of surface area to weight.

THIS MIT STUDENT FLEW 165 YARDS OF SILVER MYLAR ON A HOOP FRAME, BUT YOU WOULD NEED A HILL AND LOTS OF FRIENDS TO GATHER IT IN.
I SAW THIS FELLOW AT THE GREAT BOSTON KITE FESTIVAL FLYING A TINY TETRAHEDRON.

PLASTIC BAG SLED KITE

Flies indoors and out!

YOU WILL NEED:

PLASTIC BAG • RULER • SCISSORS • TWO 16" STICKS OR DOWELS • TAPE • KITE STRING • RAGS • WIND!

1. Cut kite pattern out of plastic. It can be bigger or smaller, but use the proportions shown here.
2. Tape 2 sticks from X to Y.
3. Attach string for bridle at A and B. Bridle should be twice the width of the kite.
4. Make loop at center of bridle string C, and tie on flying string.
5. Decorate, and tape on 3 or 5 rag tails.
6. Find a wind or run fast!

Note: it is hard to draw on plastic. But once you've built a model that flies well, next time you can make a paper or cloth kite. This model is a sure flyer.

TWISTING

Lots of people don't stop and think about how things are made and why.

I wouldn't devote a page to twisting if I hadn't witnessed hundreds of times the excitement of schoolchildren who had just learned how to make twist belts.

It is too simple to believe, yet it is a true discovery. All you need is some yarn.

For a belt, use:
5 or more strands of yarn (different colors) 4 times your waist measure.

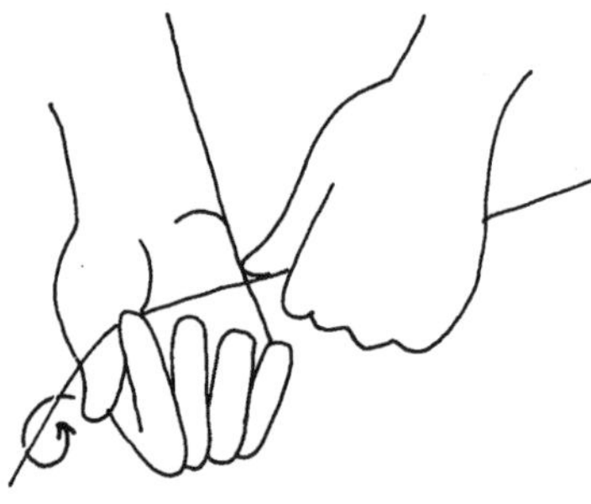

1. Attach one end of the yarn strands to a hook, knob, or anything stable.
2. Twist the other ends, keeping tension between the stable end and the twisting end.
3. When twist is good and tight, hold the twisted strands taut with one hand.
4. Find and pinch the center with the other hand.
5. Keeping everything taut, bend A to B.
6. Tie A and B together.
7. Let go of the center, and the strands will spin together in a double reverse twist that will stay put if you knot the tassel end.

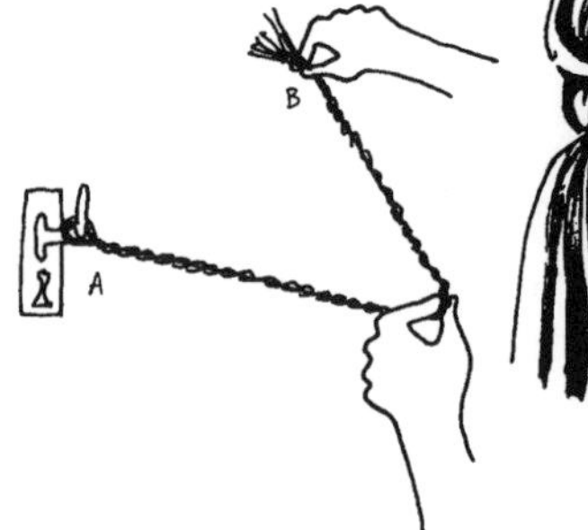

P.S. Twisted string has double strength!

ROPE WINDING

This little contraption is an "automatic" rope winder.

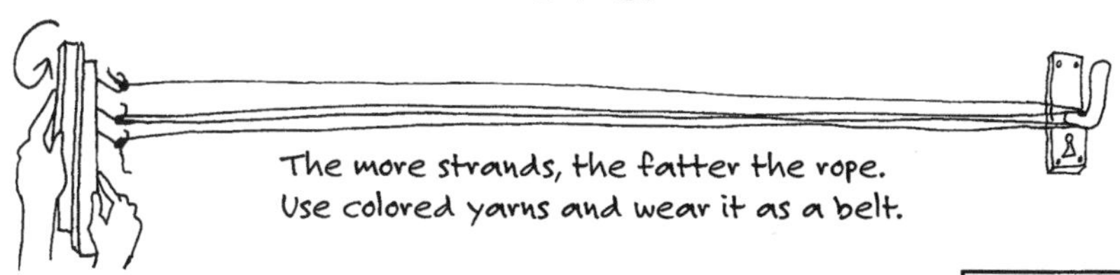

The more strands, the fatter the rope. Use colored yarns and wear it as a belt.

1. Sand wood blocks.
2. Clamp wood blocks together, and drill 3 holes $1\frac{1}{2}$" apart starting 1" from the end.
3. Cut 3 equal sections of coat hanger wire about $5\frac{1}{4}$" long
4. Bend a 1"-long foot in each wire carefully and exact.
5. Poke wires through first block until foot rests flat on block.
6. Bend wires back against underside in a zigzag.
7. Thread second block onto wires.
8. Bend wires backward at about a 30° angle.
9. Use pliers to form hooks.
10. Knot string or yarn onto top hook as shown. Then loop string to doorknob, back to middle hook, to doorknob, and back to bottom hook. Knot string onto bottom hook, and cut off excess.
11. Action: Hold one block in each hand, and rotate them. Keep rotating until strings are twisted tight.
12. To finish: Keeping tension, remove strings from hooks, and tie the 3 ends together. Still keeping tension, remove strings from doorknob, then let go. All the strands will spin together and stay put.

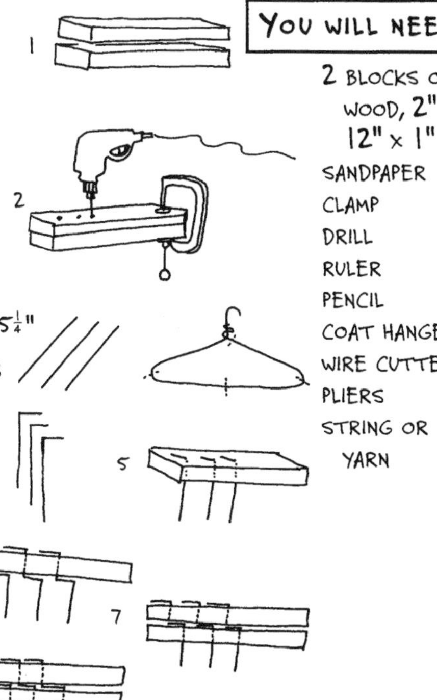

YOU WILL NEED:

2 BLOCKS OF WOOD, 2" x 12" x 1"
SANDPAPER
CLAMP
DRILL
RULER
PENCIL
COAT HANGER
WIRE CUTTERS
PLIERS
STRING OR YARN

OVER & UNDER WEAVING

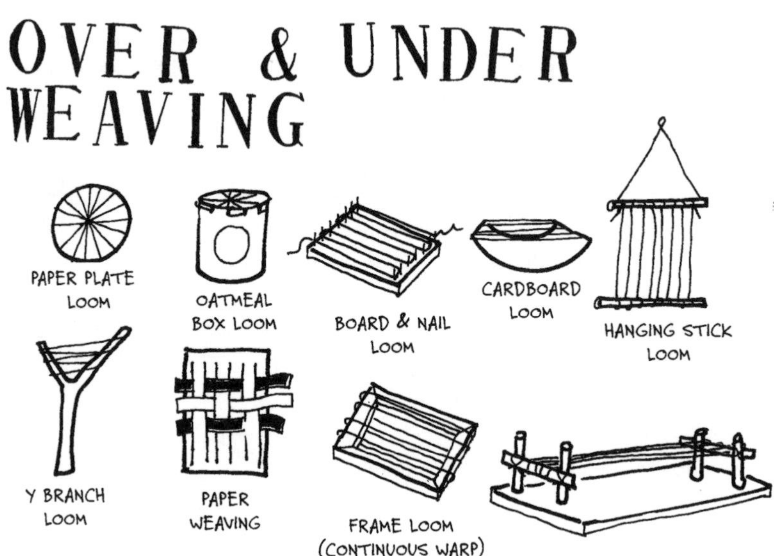

You can weave sticks, grasses, leaves, paper, string, yarn, and fingers.

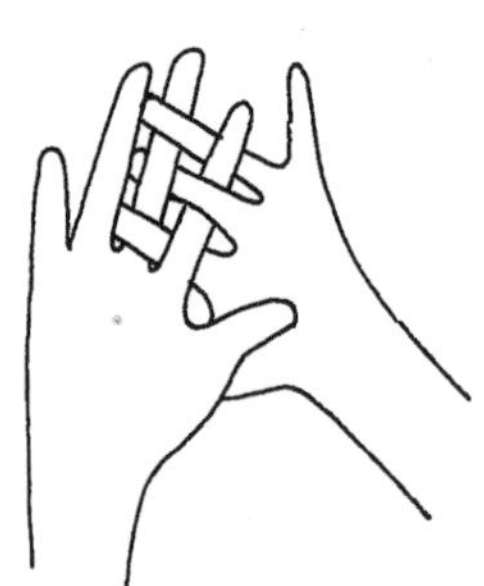

People, birds, and insects weave! Weaving is probably one of the first wonders, enabling people to make fabric for shelter, clothing to cover our tender flesh, hammocks to hang from trees, and nets and baskets to catch, carry, and keep things in.

Note: All round looms must have an odd number of strings.

PLASTIC DRINKING STRAW BELT LOOM

The first looms of this type were made of natural straw or bamboo. But we can use plastic drinking straws, available free at many fast-food places or cheap at the grocery store.

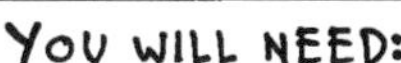

YOU WILL NEED:

4 OR 5 STRAWS • 4 OR 5 LENGTHS OF STRING TWICE YOUR WAIST SIZE

• TAPE • YARN

1. Thread or suck a string up each straw.
2. Tape one end of each string to its straw, so it won't pull down and out.
3. Tie bottom string ends in a tassel (A).
4. Tie yarn to first straw (B).
5. Work the yarn over and under straws.

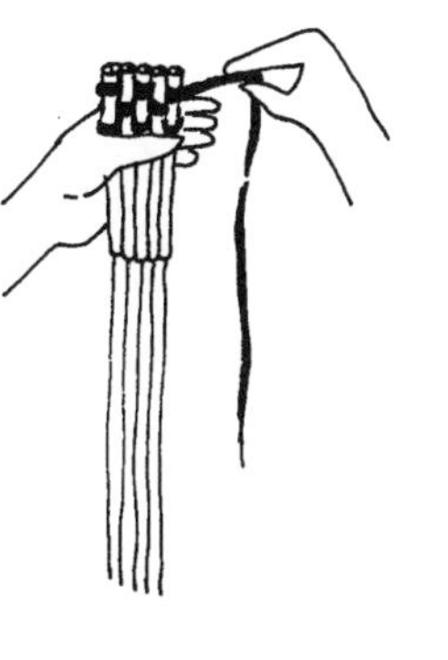

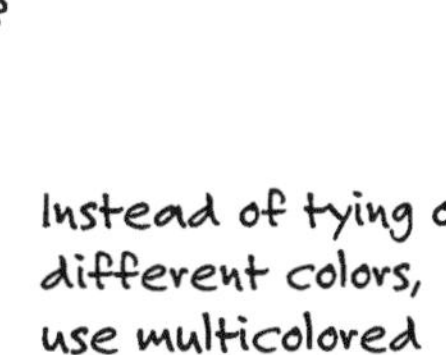

Instead of tying on different colors, use multicolored variegated yarn for instant patterns.

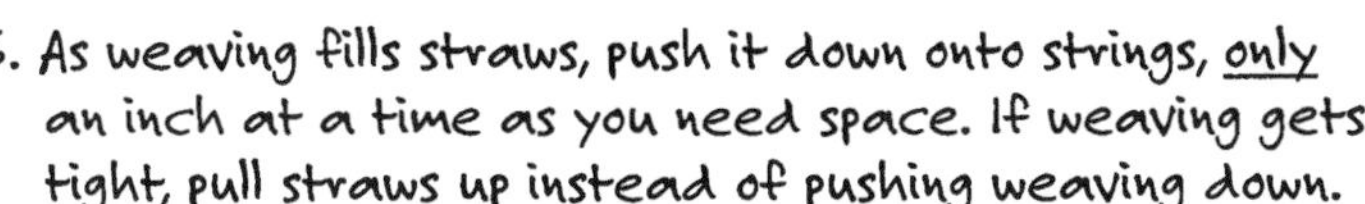

6. As weaving fills straws, push it down onto strings, only an inch at a time as you need space. If weaving gets tight, pull straws up instead of pushing weaving down.
7. At the end, push weaving off straws, and tie all ends together in a tassel.

THE HEDDLE

Boredom has always forced people to find new and better ways of doing things.

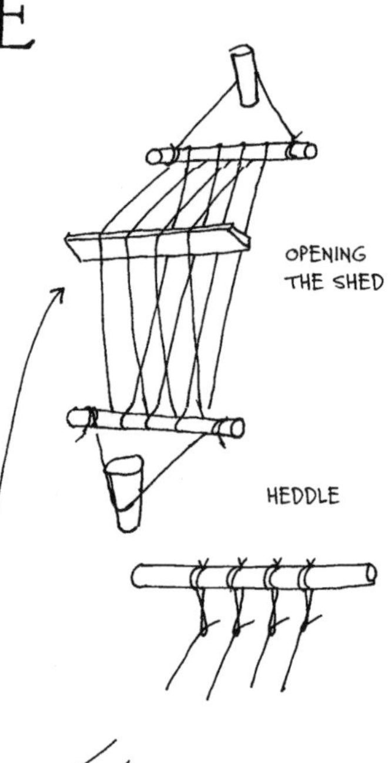

Someone said, "Ho-hum, how can I speed this up?" and with a little ingenious logic, invented the heddle.

By opening the shed, the heddle made it possible to go over one set of strings and under the other set in one easy motion. The problem was how to open the opposite shed, to go over and under the opposite set of strings, and how to then alternate sheds in turn.

2 HEDDLE BARS WITH LOOPS

The solution was 2 heddle bars with loops.

All looms can be fitted with heddles, and to share this wonderful discovery, you must try the Popsicle stick heddle loom and the box-and-stick inkle loom on pages 91 and 92.

POPSICLE STICK HEDDLE LOOM

YOU WILL NEED:

7 POPSICLE STICKS • TAPE • DRILL • COLORED STRING OR YARN • GLUE • BELT • NEEDLE

1. Tape 5 Popsicle sticks in a stack. Drill 3 holes: in the top, middle, and bottom of the sticks.
2. Tape remaining 2 sticks together, and drill 5 holes, allowing for $\frac{1}{4}$" between cross sticks.
3. Lash sticks together as shown. (Glue will hold sticks to crossbar, but the lashing method is stronger.)
4. Measure 9 warp strings 2 yards long. Thread one through each slot and one through each hole.

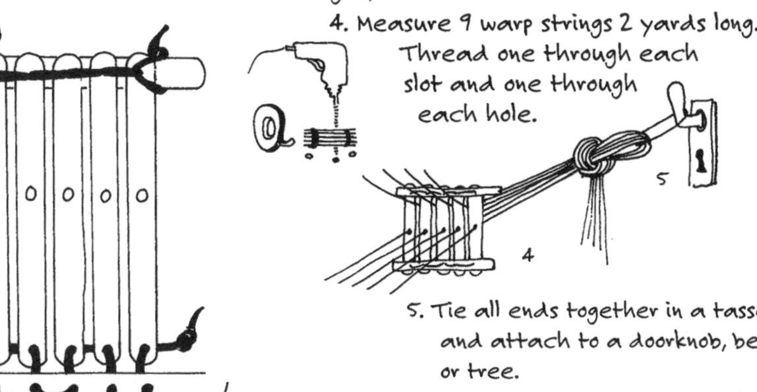

5. Tie all ends together in a tassel, and attach to a doorknob, bedpost, or tree.
6. Tie the other end to your belt, (buckled in back).
7. Sit comfortably. Pull heddle toward your belt, and raise it. Pass weaving yarn through upper shed right to left.
8. Lower heddle. Pass yarn back through lower shed left to right.

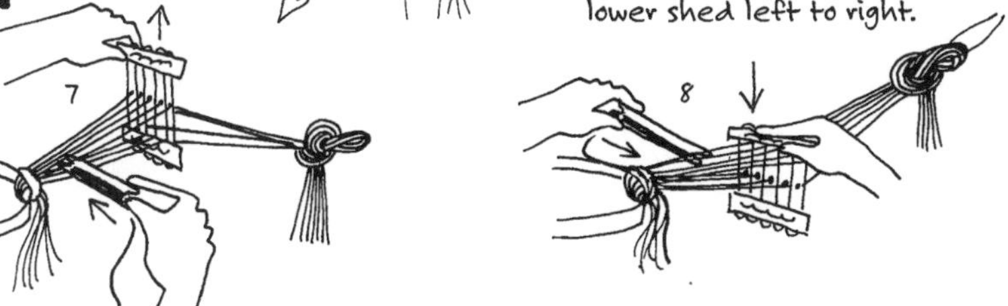

9. Continue weaving — heddle up, heddle down — until you can't reach. Then wind woven part around belt and weave on.
10. When woven belt is long enough, remove heddle and tie warp and weaving strings in a tassel at both ends. Voilà — your belt is ready to wear.

BOX & STICK INKLE LOOM

In order to make heddle looms available to hundreds of children in public schools without an art budget, we adapted the common corrugated packing box as shown here. Every child could make and own an inkle loom at no cost.

YOU WILL NEED:

CORRUGATED CARDBOARD BOX APPROXIMATELY 12" x 12" x 18" • 5 STICKS OR 3/4" DOWELS 2" WIDER THAN BOX • MAT KNIFE OR SERRATED KITCHEN KNIFE

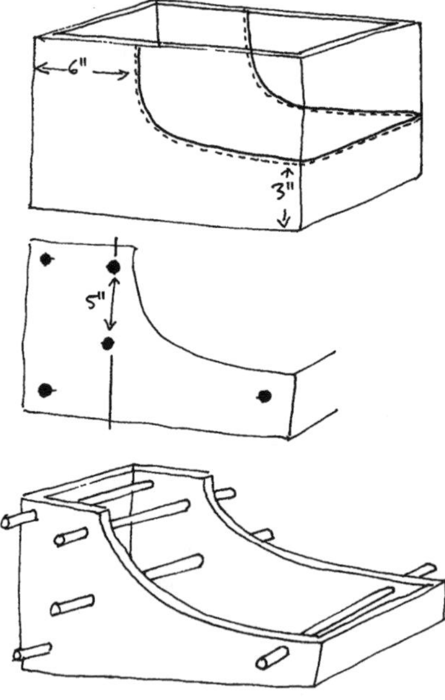

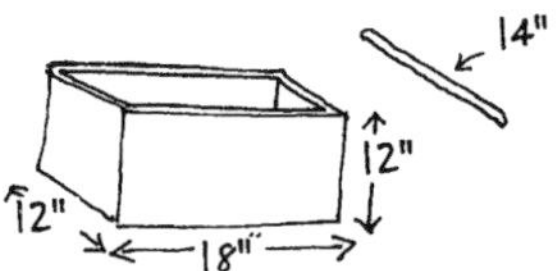

1. Cut box as shown. Trace the first side cutout onto the other side so they match.
2. Cut 5 small X's on each side to poke the sticks through. Be sure the left and right side X's match. (Allow margins for strength.) Poke sticks through X's. (The X's will make tighter holes than round cuts would.)

Note: With a little adjustment, you can adapt boxes of other dimensions.

TYING HEDDLE LOOPS

For Belts or Sashes

1. In order to make 3 equal loops, tie 3 loops as shown around bars 2 and 3. Then slip the bars out and remove the loops.
2. Double each loop, and slip all 3 over bar 2 (the heddle bar).

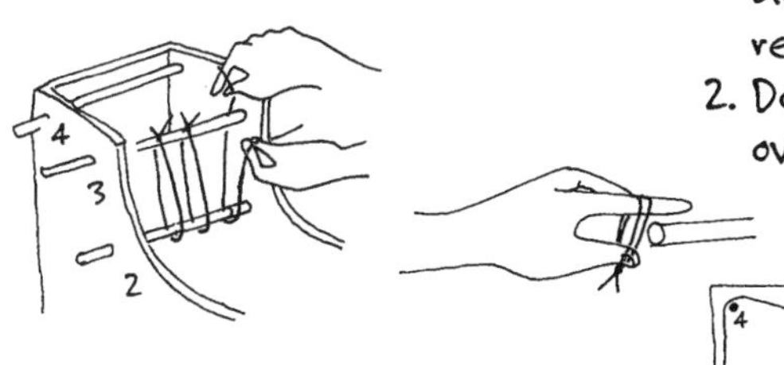

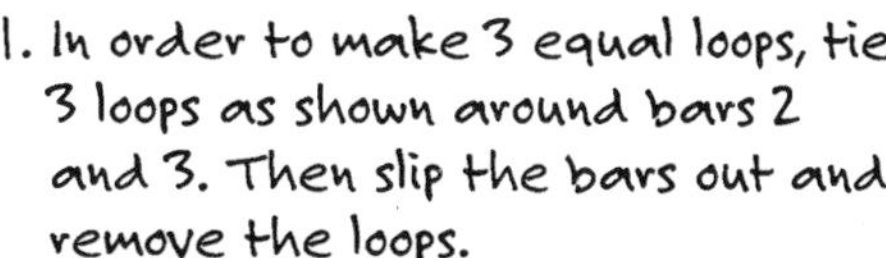

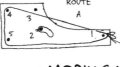

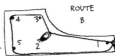

WARPING YOUR LOOM

3. Cut 6 strings about 48" long.
4. Follow route A for the first string and route B for the second, then continue alternating each string.

   All the A strings go from bar 1 to bar 4, under bar 5, under bar 1, and tie in a bow.

   All the B strings go from bar 2, through <u>double</u> heddle loops on bar 2, over bars 3 and 4, under bars 5 and 1, and tie in a bow.

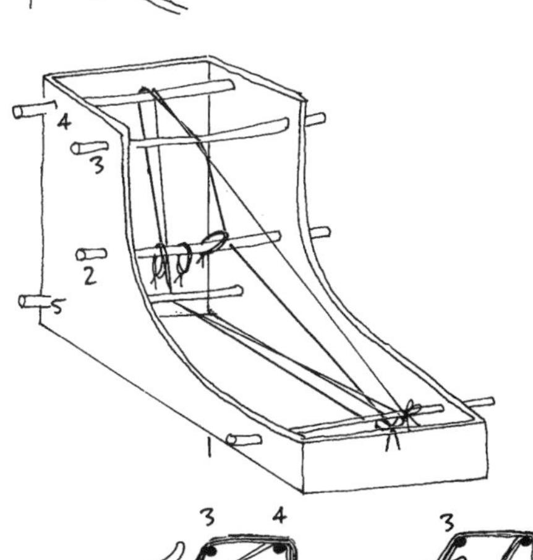

RAISE

TO WEAVE

Raise and lower sheds with finger:

5. Raise strings under bar 3, and pass weaving yarn through shed <u>right to left</u>.
6. Lower strings under bar 3, and pass yarn through shed <u>left to right</u>.
7. Continue alternating raising and lowering until woven part is 3" or 4" long. Slide woven part backward toward bar 5. When woven part reaches bar 3, untie warp bows. Remove weaving from loom. Tie a tassel at both ends, and wear it!

THRUMMING LOOM

FOR SCRAPS OF MATERIAL TO MAKE A RAG TAIL RUG

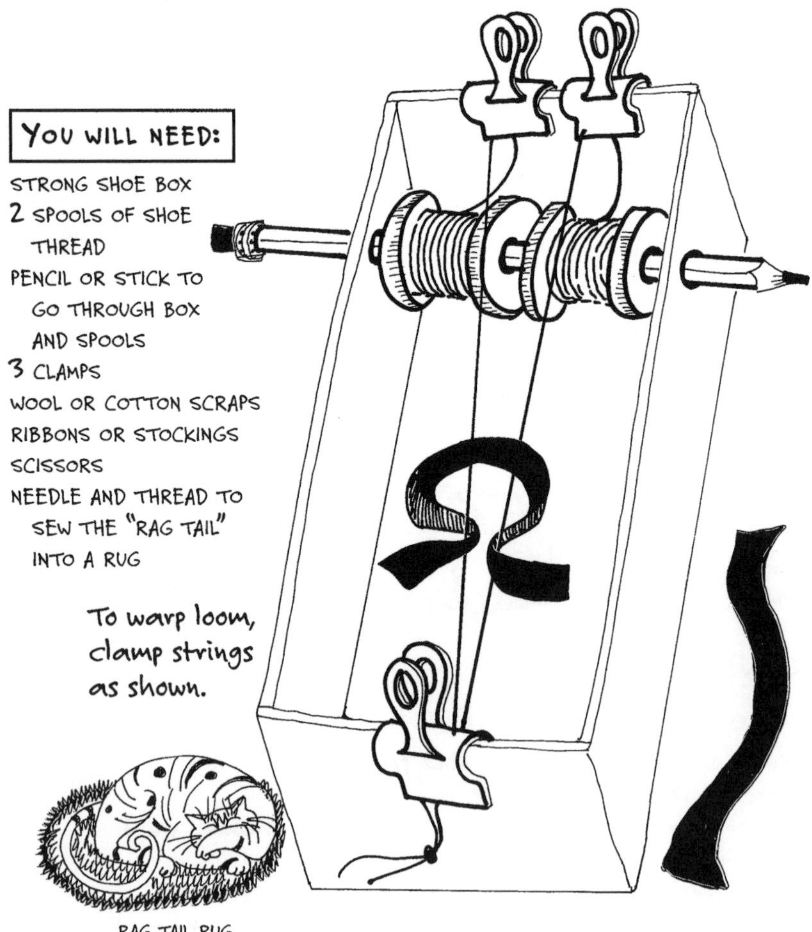

YOU WILL NEED:

STRONG SHOE BOX
2 SPOOLS OF SHOE THREAD
PENCIL OR STICK TO GO THROUGH BOX AND SPOOLS
3 CLAMPS
WOOL OR COTTON SCRAPS
RIBBONS OR STOCKINGS
SCISSORS
NEEDLE AND THREAD TO SEW THE "RAG TAIL" INTO A RUG

To warp loom, clamp strings as shown.

1. Tear or cut $\frac{1}{2}$"-wide strips of cloth.
2. Wrap strips around your hand, and cut strips along top edge. (This is a quick way to measure equal scraps.) 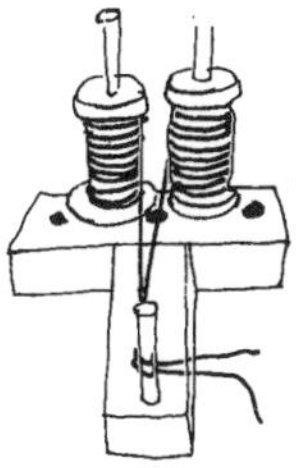
3. Hitch each piece around warp strings, and pull down to tighten the knot.
4. As you finish a foot or two, sew knots into a circle. (See cat rug.)

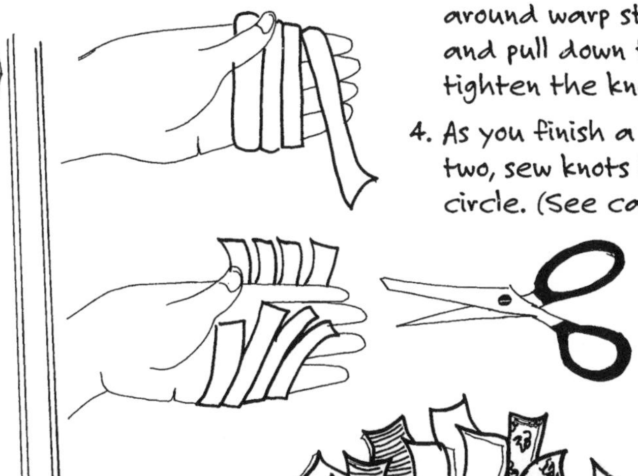

Or make a permanent wooden thrumming loom with movable dowels.

WEAVING IN MATH CLASS

Try warping your loom and assigning a number to each string. Then mutter the over-under song as you weave back and forth and think about odds and evens: "Under, odd. Over, even."

SKIP-COUNTING ON 9 STRINGS

Now go on to skip-counting, picking up every third string. Start with the 3rd string, then the 6th string, then the 9th, going from left to right. An easy way to learn the times tables.

On the next row, pick up every third string, too: 7, 4, and 1, going from right to left. See what pattern it makes.

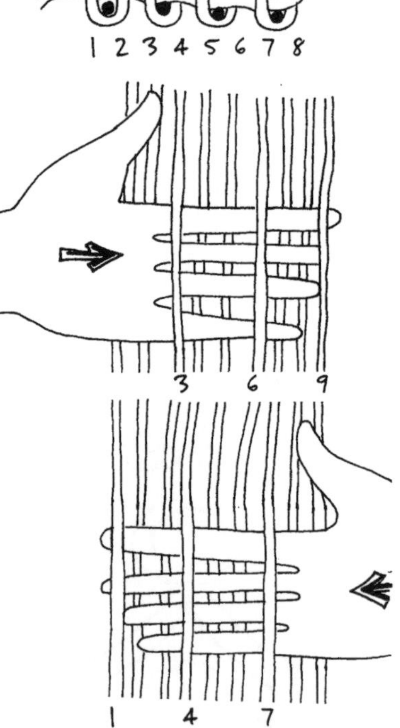

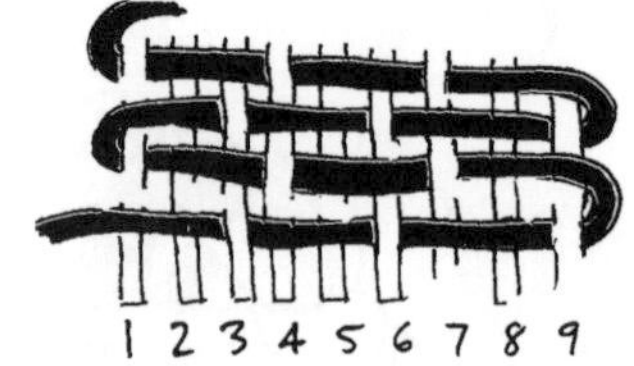

Try all kinds of combinations — it's hand-logic math.

SQUARE NUMBER WEAVING

ALGEBRA AND THE BINOMIAL THEOREM IN 2 DIMENSIONS

$$(\text{red} + \text{black})^2 = \text{red}^2 + 2\ \text{red/black} + \text{black}^2$$

OR

$$(a + b)^2 = a^2 + 2ab + b^2$$

1. Warp 8 red and 4 black strings (or multiples, such as 32 red and 16 black).

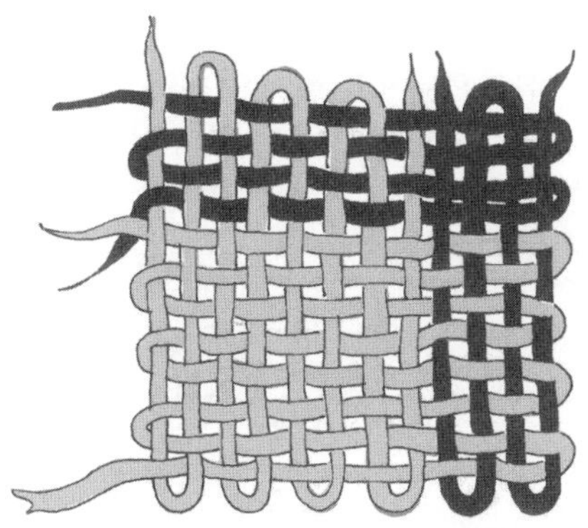

2. Weave 8 red rows and then 4 black rows.
3. What do you see?
   What did you prove?

Right: $(a + b)^2 = a^2 + 2ab + b^2$ — the binomial theorem

WEAVING PATTERNS

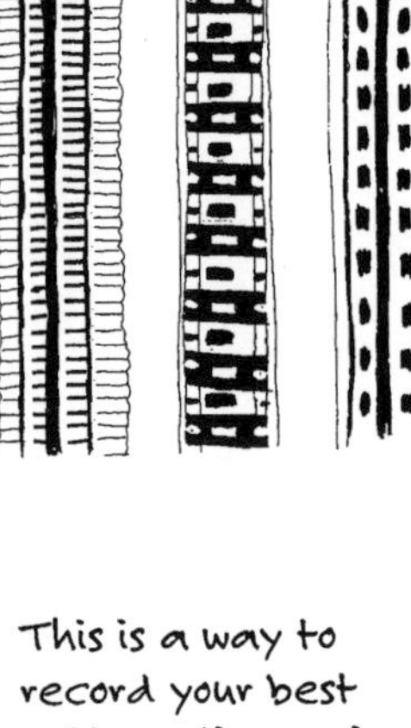

Many exciting effects can be achieved simply by arranging color patterns in the warping of your loom.

1. Using <u>random</u> colors as well as thick and thin yarn and ribbons produces endless surprises. (Torn rags work nicely.)
2. <u>Stripes</u> are produced by using 3 or more strands of the same color: 6 red, 6 black, 6 white, 6 black, 6 red, or many variations thereof. . . .
3. <u>Designs</u>: with 2 colors: 5 of color A, 1 of color B, 5 A, 2 B, 5 A, 1 B, 5 A . . . or many variations.
4. <u>Classic Patterns</u>: such as 3 A, 2 B, AC, AC, AC (8 or 10 times), 2 B, 3 A.

Try 23 strands of knitting yarn = 1 inch

This is a way to record your best pattern discoveries. Experiment with materials such as ribbons, yarn, cord, and fabric strips. Substitute any colors you like.

WARP-FACE BELT PATTERN

TRADITIONAL PATTERNS USING FINE COTTON OR LINEN

44 Warp Strings
Weave with white.
8 white
4 red
1 white } 6 times
1 black }
1 white
7 red
Then reverse.

38 Warp Strings
Weave with white.
5 white
4 black
1 white } 3 times
1 black }
1 white
5 black
1 white } 6 times
1 red }
Then reverse.

40 Warp Strings
Weave with white.
3 white
3 black
4 white
1 red } 2 times
1 white }
1 red
4 white
3 black
Then reverse.

WEED WEAVING

ON NATURAL STRUCTURES

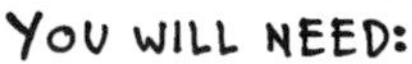

STICKS OR BRANCHES
• STRING • SCISSORS
• NATURAL MATERIALS

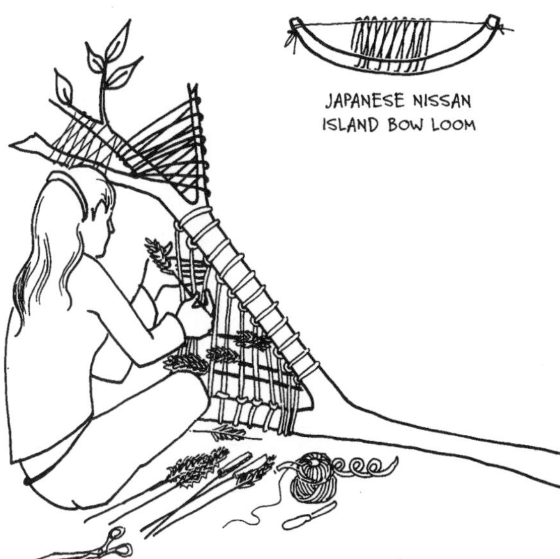

Look for driftwood, Queen Anne's lace, wheat, long stalks, all kinds of grasses and dry weeds, milkweed, cattails, vetch, vines, flotsam, kelp, fibers, feathers, corn husks, leaves, bark, bamboo, or reeds.

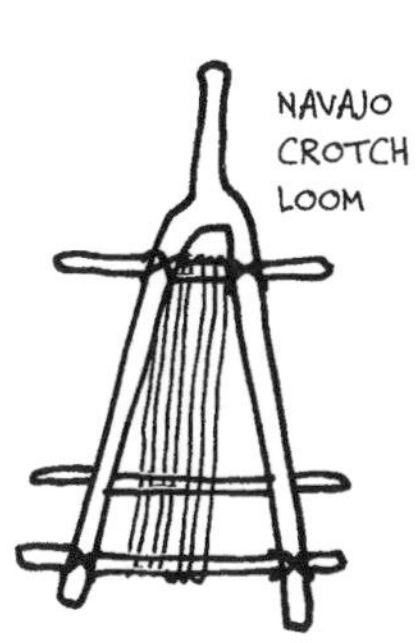

When my son Piet was four, he made a web of yarn and strings all around his room that only he was small enough to pass through.

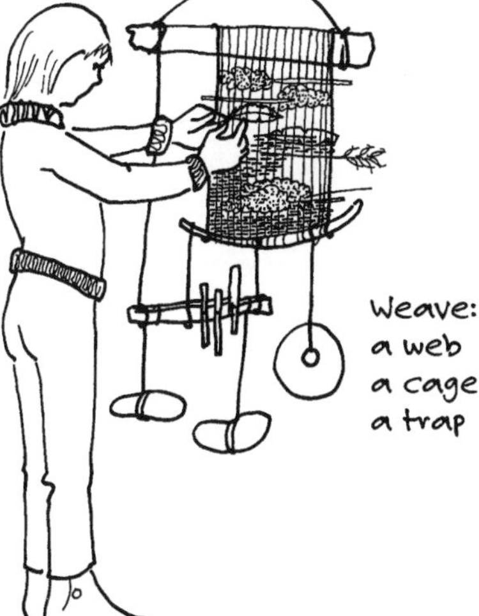

Weave:
a web
a cage
a trap

TWINING

A PURSE OR POUCH

YOU WILL NEED:

FRAME (MAKE ONE, OR BUY A PAINTING STRETCHER.) • GOOD STRONG CORD • STRING OR YARN • SCISSORS

WARPING

1. Tie cord around frame twice. Tie a bow, leaving long tails.
2. Cut warp strings about 1 yard long, and hitch each onto the frame cord as shown at right.

Tie warp strings around front, corners, and back of frame.

TWINING

3. Using 2 balls of string or yarn (same or different colors) and starting anywhere, catch twining yarn around 2 warp strings, then twist yarn and catch the next 2 warp strings into the opening.
4. Twist yarn again, and continue catching and twisting yarn around warp strings, changing colors as you choose.
5. When you have twined enough, leaving at least 3" at the bottom, remove work from frame.
6. Close the bottom of the pouch by sewing or tying tails together.

Keep pushing the twining yarn up tight so the rows look tidy and even. Go round and round.

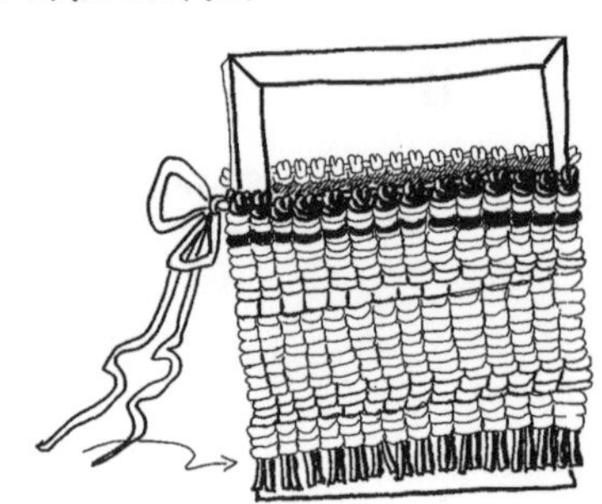

STRING BAG SHOULDER STRAP

TUBULAR TWINING

7. Untie the cord bow.
8. Tie alternating knots, right over left, left over right, all the way to the end.
9. Tie end to the other side of the bag.

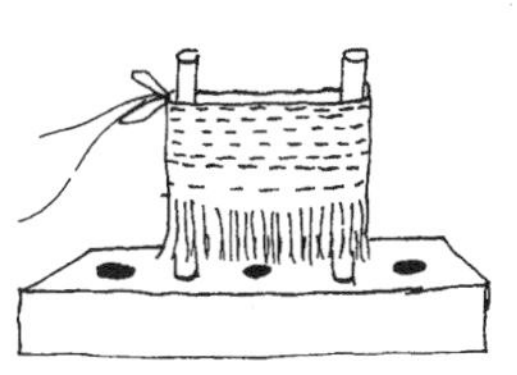

P.S. HERE IS A TWINING LOOM MADE OUT OF A 2" x 4" BLOCK OF WOOD WITH 1" DOWELS. DRILL 4 OR MORE 1"-DIAMETER HOLES FOR WIDER OR NARROWER WORK.

Right over left

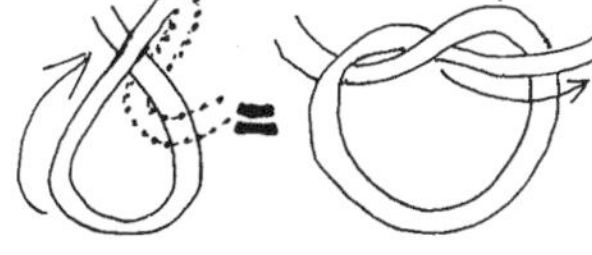

Left over right

If you don't like tassels, sew bag together inside out to hide them.

MACRAMÉ KNOTS

OR SAILORS' LACE

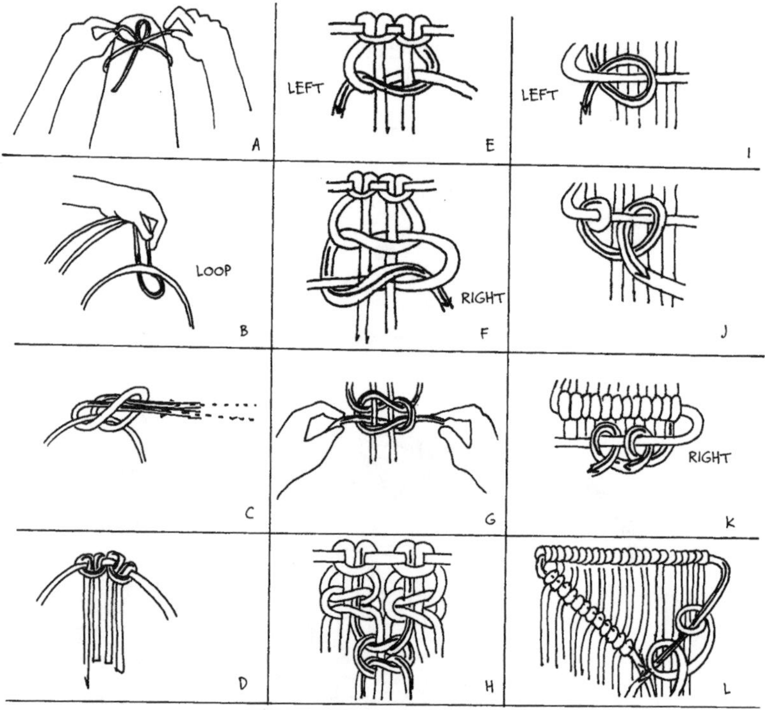

<u>The knee harness</u> is very comfortable for small work.

A. Tie holding cord around your knee. Slide bow to back of leg.

B–D. Hitch strings to cord in even numbers. Beginners could start with 2 strings 24" long. Hitch the loop middle to the holding cord.

<u>The square knot</u> has a left and a right part around the 2 center strings.

E. Right over left.

F. Left over right.

G. Pull square knot into shape.

H. Shows how you join strings on second row.

<u>The half hitch</u> must be double to hold tight. A row of half hitches can be set horizontally or diagonally.

I. The left outside string acts as crossbar.

J. Each string hitches around crossbar twice.

K. To hitch from right side, reverse method.

L. Hitching on a diagonal.

EASY 4-STRING

MACRAMÉ BELT

YOU WILL NEED:

HEAVY MASON'S TWINE OR VENETIAN BLIND CORD • RULER OR MEASURING TAPE • SCISSORS

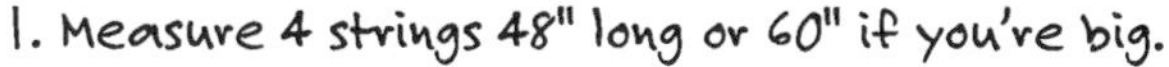

1. Measure 4 strings 48" long or 60" if you're big.
2. Tie a tassel to hold the 4 strings together.
3. Hold tassel between your toes, or tie it to a chair or your knee.
4. Hold the 2 middle strings in your teeth or on your belt.
5. Tie square knots as shown in figures E, F, and G on preceding page.
6. About halfway down, switch strings. Continue knotting with long strings on the outside, short ones in your teeth or on your belt.

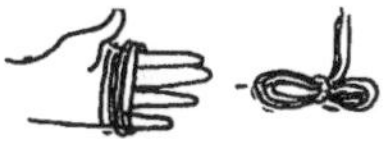

If 48" of string is too hard to handle, tie it in a butterfly and let it out as you need more string.

The spiral is made by tying only half square knots all the way down (figure E or F). Let it turn over as you go. Switch to short strings midway.

YOU WILL NEED: THIN MASON'S TWINE • RULER OR MEASURING TAPE • SCISSORS • BEADS (OPTIONAL)

MACRAMÉ NECKLACE SAMPLER

1. Cut 9 strings 30" long.
2. Tie one string around your knee. Slide bow knot to back of leg.
3. Hitch the other 8 strings onto the knee string as in figure D, page 102.
4. Tie 3 rows of square knots across. 1st and 3rd rows will have 4 square knots. 2nd row will have only 3.
5. Using left outside string, tie 2 rows of half hitches, going right, then left, as in figures I, J, and K, page 102.
6. Spiral on each 4 strings, making 4 spirals about 1" long.

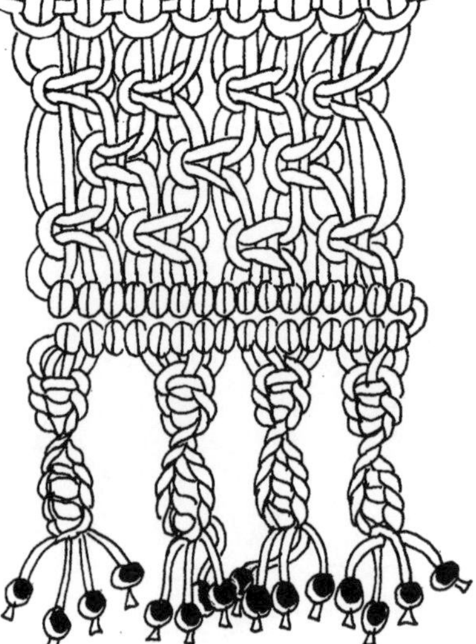

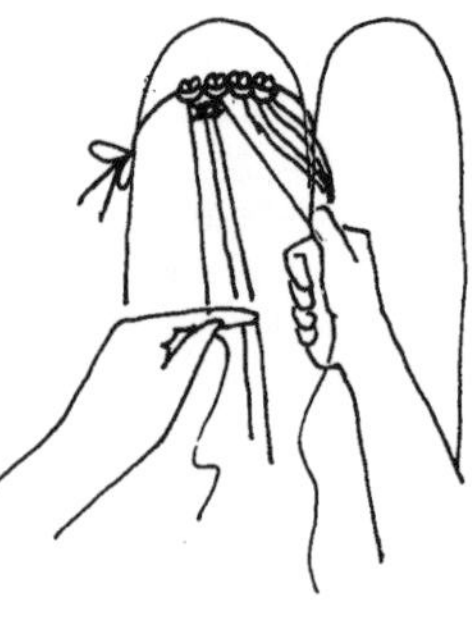

If you have beads that fit your string, thread them on the neck string and at the ends of the spirals.

YOU WILL NEED: MEDIUM FINE LINEN OR COTTON CROCHET TWINE • RULER OR MEASURING TAPE • SCISSORS

LOVE POUCH

FOR LITTLE MACRAMÉ EXPERTS

1. Cut one string 90" long, and tie it around your knee.
2. Cut 27 strings 32" long, and hitch them onto the knee string.
3. Cut one string 60" long, and hitch it onto knee string at far left so half of it is the same length as the others and the rest gives you a long string for hitching crossbars.
4. Now you have 56 strings all 16" long except the crossbar hitching string.
5. Make 2 rows of double half hitches from left to right and back again.
6. Make 3 rows of square knots.
7. Make 2 rows of double half hitches.
8. Make 13 rows of square knots.
9. Make 2 rows of double half hitches.

10. Make 3 rows of square knots.
11. Untie holding cord from knee, and fold macramé in half. Find center of holding string, and pull gently until you have equal parts on both sides of pouch. Tie onto knee.
12. Using the long crossbar string, make 2 rows of double half hitches on every other string, thus closing the bottom.
13. Sew up open side of pouch.
14. Neck string: Tie knots on holding strings, one left, one right, all the way up on each side. Then tie them all together.

KNOTS

Overhand Knot

Figure Eight Knot

Square Knot

Granny Knot

Sheet Bend Knot

Bowline

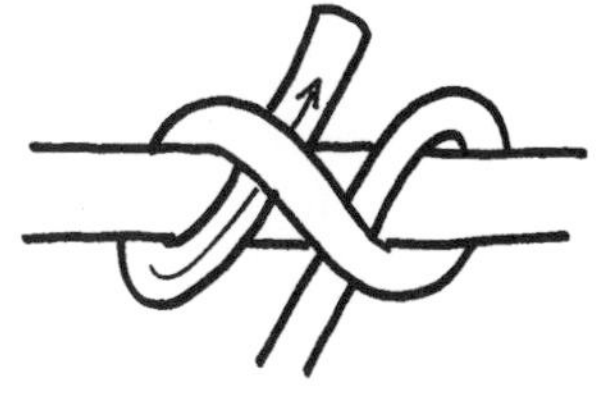

Clove Hitch

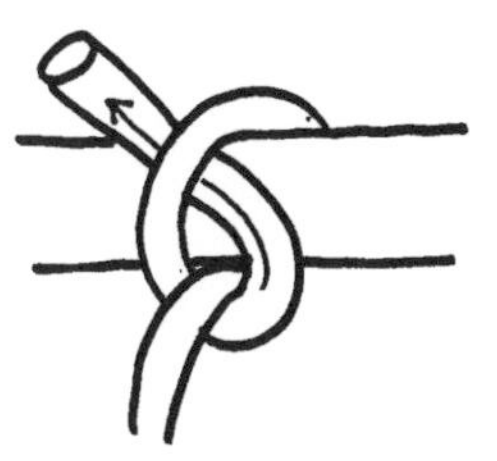

Timber Hitch

Package Knot

Fisherman's Knot or Joining Knot

COMMANDO'S VEST

This is an authentic World War II British Commando's thermal vest — warm in winter, cool in summer.

YOU WILL NEED:

$\frac{1}{2}$" OR $\frac{3}{4}$" DOWEL (OR 2 STRAIGHT STICKS ABOUT 16" LONG) • KNIFE • PENCIL SHARPENER • SANDPAPER • RUBBER BANDS • ABOUT 150 YARDS COTTON MASON'S TWINE #18

KNITTING NEEDLES

1. Cut dowel in half. Sharpen one end of each half, and smooth them with sandpaper.
2. Wrap rubber bands onto blunt ends.

VEST

Make 2 sides, front and back the same.

3. Cast on 25 stitches.
4. Knit 30 rows.
5. Armhole: Decrease 1 stitch at end of each row for 7 rows.
6. Knit remaining 18 stitches for 12 rows.
7. Cast off loosely.
8. Sew up sides to armhole.
9. Tie shoulders together.

Gauge:
1" = 2 rows
on $\frac{1}{2}$" dowels

If you don't know how to knit, ask someone to teach you.

YOU WILL NEED: FABRIC • MEASURING TAPE • PENCIL • SCISSORS • PINS • NEEDLE AND THREAD • BIAS TAPE (OPTIONAL)

QUICK CLOTHES

BASIC CAFTAN-COAT-DRESS-ROBE-SHIRT

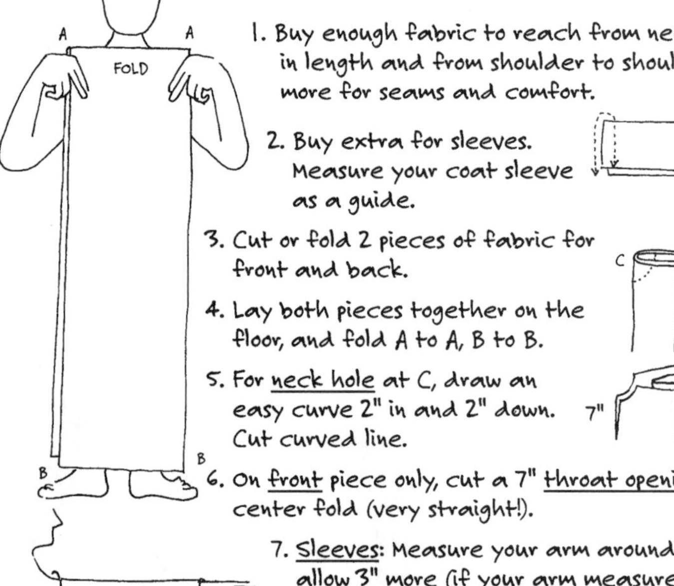

1. Buy enough fabric to reach from neck to feet in length and from shoulder to shoulder plus 2" more for seams and comfort.
2. Buy extra for sleeves. Measure your coat sleeve as a guide.
3. Cut or fold 2 pieces of fabric for front and back.
4. Lay both pieces together on the floor, and fold A to A, B to B.
5. For <u>neck hole</u> at C, draw an easy curve 2" in and 2" down. Cut curved line.
6. On <u>front</u> piece only, cut a 7" <u>throat opening</u> on center fold (very straight!).
7. <u>Sleeves</u>: Measure your arm around shoulder, and allow 3" more (if your arm measures 14" around, cut your sleeves 17") x however long your arm is or you want your sleeve to be. Add a <u>gusset</u> under arm if sleeve is binding.
8. <u>Sew</u> dress/caftan together at shoulders (unless it's already together because fabric was folded lengthwise).
9. <u>Sew</u> sleeves in place.
10. <u>Sew</u> side seams from wrist to underarm, curving gently, on down to knee. Leave the rest open to floor as a "walking slit."

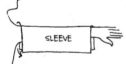

11. Hem sleeves, walking slit, bottom edges, neck, and throat.

A. Easiest way: Fray edges.

B. Easy way: Buy bias binding of a complementary color, and sew it onto all the raw edges, either letting it show like piping or turning it under as an inner facing.

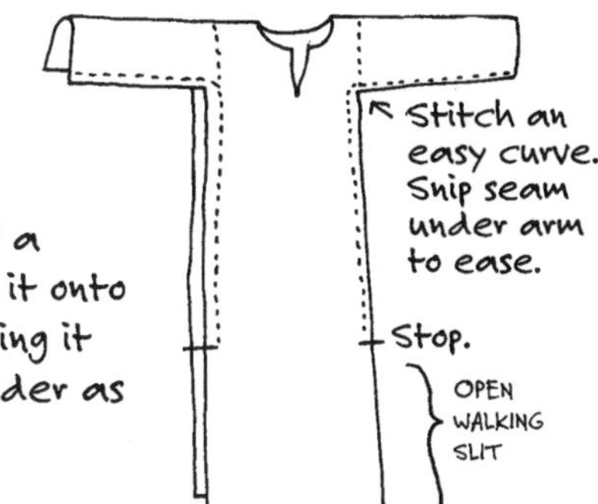

Variations and Adaptations

This basic model can become:

What more could you need?

YOU WILL NEED: FABRIC • MEASURING TAPE • SCISSORS • PINS • NEEDLE AND THREAD

BODY LOGIC CLOTHES

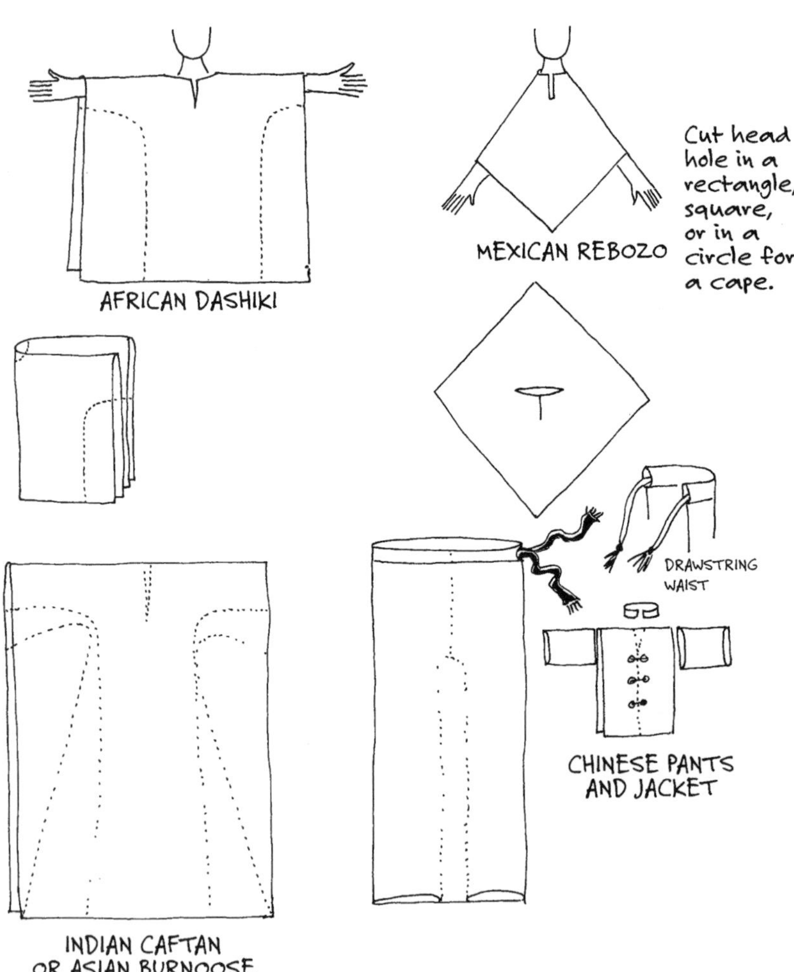

Cut head hole in a rectangle, square, or in a circle for a cape.
DRAWSTRING WAIST

AFRICAN DASHIKI

MEXICAN REBOZO

INDIAN CAFTAN OR ASIAN BURNOOSE

CHINESE PANTS AND JACKET

MONIQUE'S BODY-LOGIC STRAIGHT SKIRT

YOU WILL NEED:

FABRIC • MEASURING TAPE • SCISSORS • NEEDLE AND THREAD • IRON • ZIPPER • GROSGRAIN RIBBON

When I was a student living in Paris, I learned a lot about the logic of simple economical patterns for body covering.

Necessity is the mother of improvisation, and the French are thrifty and clever.

While I was bicycling through the château country, Monique invited me to visit her home in the Loire Valley. We had picked up fabrics in the marketplace and wanted to make skirts. "Patterns are for people who don't understand body logic," she explained.

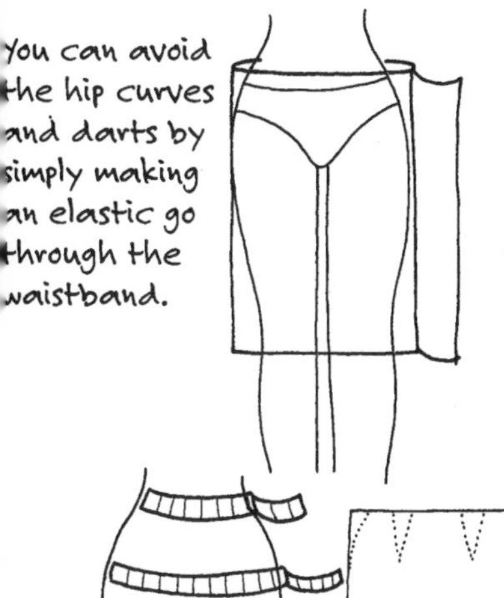

You can avoid the hip curves and darts by simply making an elastic go through the waistband.

1. Since your hips are the widest part of you, wrap fabric around your hips like a straight tube to determine the width of your skirt. All hips curve, so cut a slow curve at both sides.
2. Sew seams together except for 5" at top left, for zipper. Sew curve seam.
3. Measure your waist. Measure your hips. Adjust the difference by making 2 darts in front and 2 in back. Sew and press.
4. Sew zipper in.
5. <u>Waistband</u>: Sew ribbon to front side of skirt waist.
6. Then fold ribbon backward and stitch to inside.
7. Hem bottom. Finis!

DONUT BLOUSE

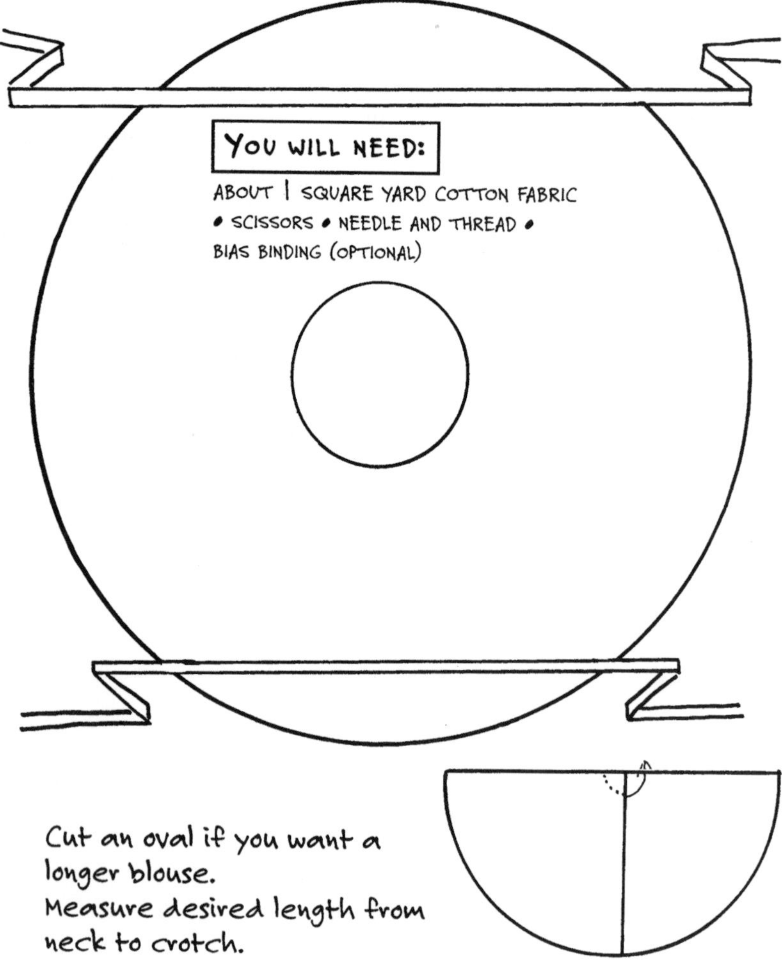

YOU WILL NEED:
ABOUT 1 SQUARE YARD COTTON FABRIC
• SCISSORS • NEEDLE AND THREAD •
BIAS BINDING (OPTIONAL)

Cut an oval if you want a longer blouse.
Measure desired length from neck to crotch.

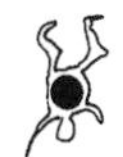

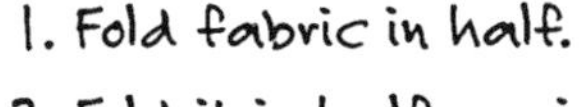

1. Fold fabric in half.
2. Fold it in half again.

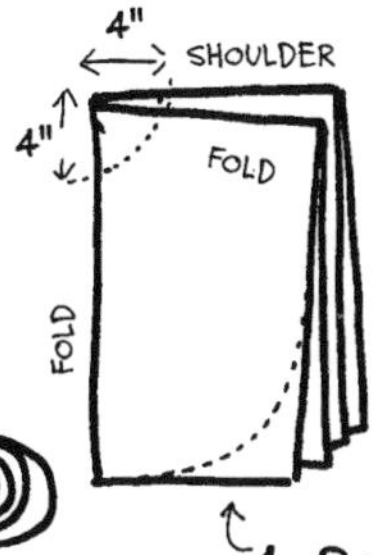

4" SHOULDER
4"
FOLD
FOLD

3. Measure 4" in at top folded corner. Cut out a 4" neck circle.

4. Round out bottom curve to make the donut.

5. Hem all edges, or trim edges with bias binding.

6. Make 2 belt strings out of fabric or bias binding.
Front belt = 1 yard
Back belt = 2 yards

7. Put the donut over your head, and pin the belts at waistline. Take donut off, and sew front and back belt in place.

Tie front belt in back. Then bring back belt around to front, and tie it in back.
If front belt makes a bump in back when tied, sew on Velcro pads and overlap ends instead.

TIE-DYE AN ANCIENT ART

The first early human to sit on a berry discovered dye. Tying came later, but when dyeing and tying got together, people noticed that the knot resisted the dye.

YOU WILL NEED: STARCH-FREE CLOTH, SUCH AS A COTTON T-SHIRT OR SHEET, OR SILK OR MUSLIN FABRIC • CLOTH DYE • WATER • BUCKET • THREAD • RUBBER BANDS

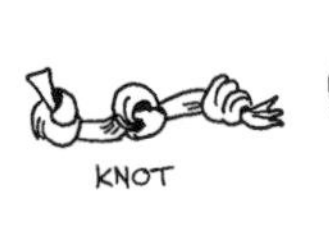

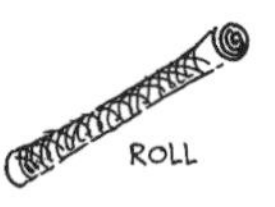

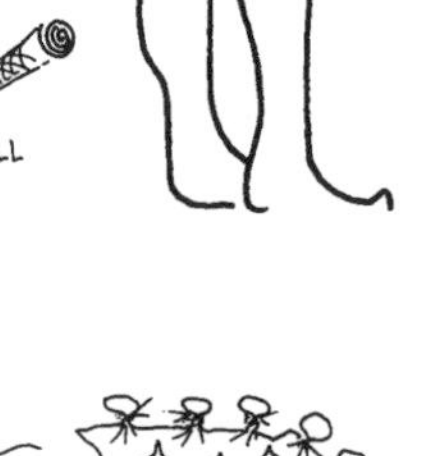

There are many ways to tie using thread or rubber bands and many ways to dye using natural or commercial dyes.

PUFF

STITCH

PINCH

PAPER TOWEL FAN-AND-FOLD DYEING

Fun for Little Beginners

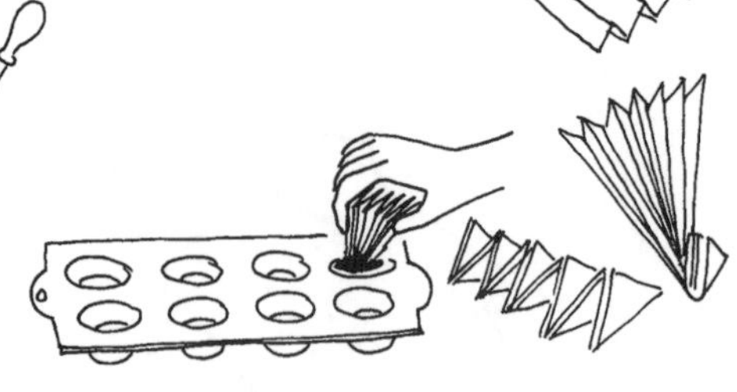

Dilute vegetable food colors in muffin tin. Fold paper towels, and dip them into dyes. Unfold towels, and let them dry. Also try eyedropper drops of food colors on wet paper towels.

Packaged dyes are easy to use. Use less water for stronger colors. Directions on package. Liquid dyes are better because they don't have granules, which can make spots. Batik dyes are more expensive but are colorfast and have stronger colors.

DYEING

Dyeing is magic, one of the oldest home arts in every culture all over the world. Every family and tribe had its own recipes.

Natural dyes come from:

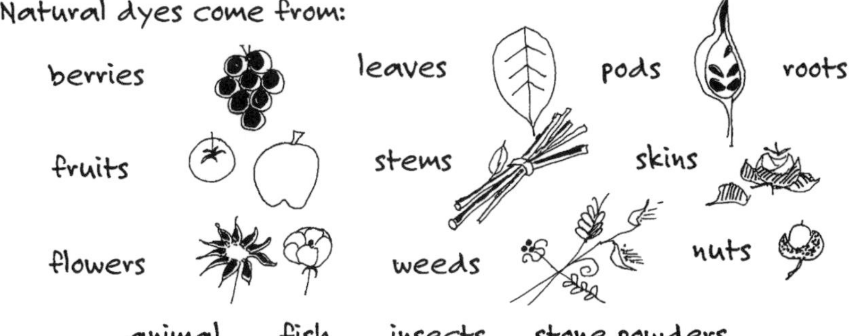

animal fish insects stone powders

See how many colors you can create.

RENDERING
(GETTING THE COLOR OUT OF DYE STUFF)

Crush berries and soak roots.
You will need 1 pound of your dye stuff per 1 pound of wool.
Boil dye stuff for 1 hour in stainless steel pan with enough water to cover dye stuff. Strain.

THESE MATERIALS:	MAKE:
ONION SKINS	BROWNISH YELLOW
BIRCH LEAVES	ANOTHER YELLOW
PRIVET BERRIES	YELLOW-GREEN
MADDER ROOT	RED
RIPE WALNUT SHELLS	BROWN (SOAK FOR 2 DAYS.)
NETTLES (2 POUNDS; IN MAY)	YELLOW-GREEN
DAHLIAS	WARM BROWNS
POISON IVY BERRIES (DANGEROUS TO GATHER BUT PROVIDE ONE OF THE FEW GOOD BLACKS)	BLACKISH

QUICK BATIK

Wax resist can be done on paper or cloth with wax crayons, melted candle stubs, paraffin, or beeswax.

CRAYON ON PAPER

1. Draw a picture or design with crayons. Press hard, and cover all the paper.
2. Scrumple up the paper.
3. Smooth it out, and paint it over with ebony stain, black ink, or thinned black poster paint. The cracking gives it a nice antique look.

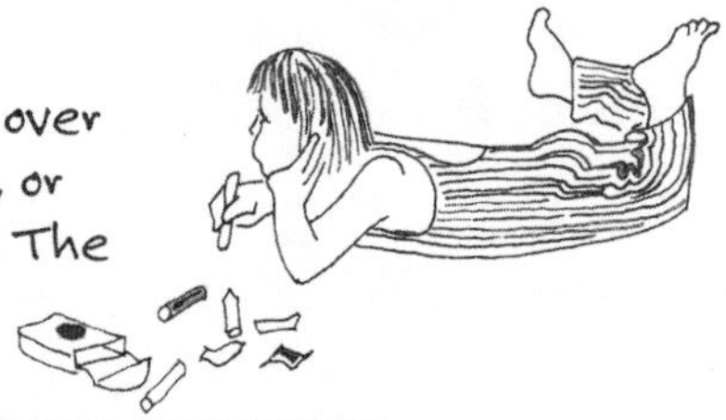

HOT WAX ON CLOTH

YOU WILL NEED:

PARAFFIN • DOUBLE BOILER • HOT PLATE • POT HOLDER • BRUSHES • WHITE OR LIGHT-COLORED COTTON FABRIC OR OLD BEDSHEET • COLD-WATER DYES • SALT • LOTS OF NEWSPAPER AND PANS • IRON

A word of caution: Heating wax can be very DANGEROUS. Always use a double boiler. Don't let it boil or smoke, and don't leave it unwatched.

1. Melt paraffin in double boiler.
2. With a good brush, paint a hot wax design on cloth. In order to resist the dye later on, it should penetrate the cloth and look transparent.
3. Prepare dyes, adding a big spoonful of salt to each color. Paint on dyes.
4. Let cloth dry. Then iron it between newspapers to remove wax.

BATIK is an ancient and noble ART with many refinements but you can get a taste of it using This QUICK Method

PLEASE Be careful

LOVE · YOU

STOCKING MASKS

YOU WILL NEED:

NYLON STOCKINGS • SCISSORS • WIRE COAT HANGERS • FABRIC SCRAPS, YARN, FELT, BUTTONS, ETC. • GLUE; OR NEEDLE AND THREAD

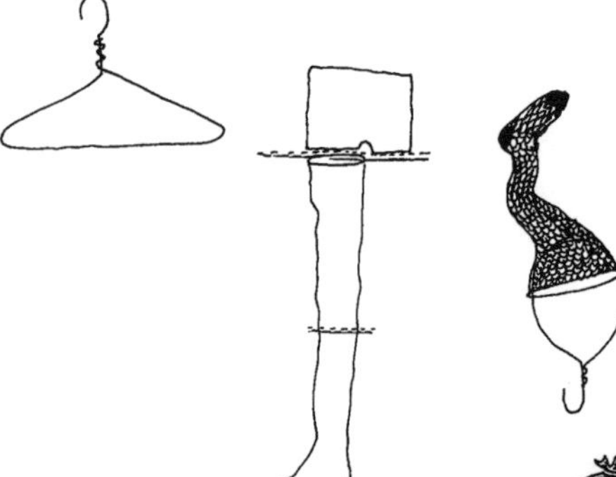

HIDING BEHIND THE MASK

Many things can be said.
Many secrets can be told.
Shyness is hidden.
If you make a bold mask,
you can tell your teacher what you think
and make suggestions to your parents.
If you make a wise and thoughtful
mask, you can explain things —
even things you didn't dare say.
If you make a new-person mask,
you can be someone new.
You can practice being different
behind a mask.

1. Cut off stocking legs. Then cut legs in half.
2. One stocking leg will make 2 masks. Tie one end of the footless section closed.
3. Pull section of stocking over rounded coat hanger. Tie at neck.
4. To make a face, sew or glue on fabric scraps, yarn, felt, buttons, etc.

BRAID WIG

YOU WILL NEED:

AN OLD PAIR OF PANTY HOSE NO LONGER GOOD FOR YOUR LEGS (HOLES, TEARS, AND RUNS WON'T SHOW ONCE LEGS ARE BRAIDED.)
SCISSORS
RUBBER BAND (OPTIONAL)

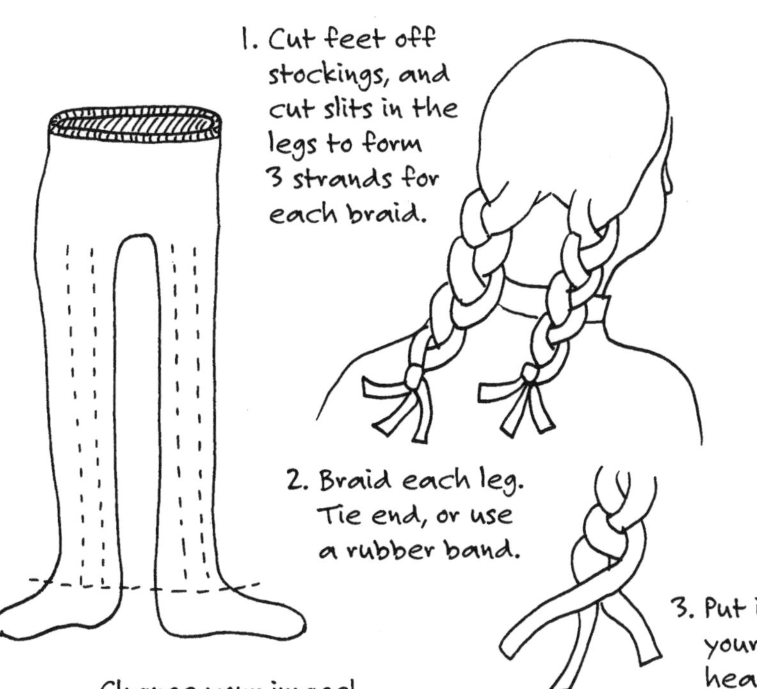

1. Cut feet off stockings, and cut slits in the legs to form 3 strands for each braid.
2. Braid each leg. Tie end, or use a rubber band.
3. Put it on your head.

Change your image!

GLOVE FINGER PUPPETS

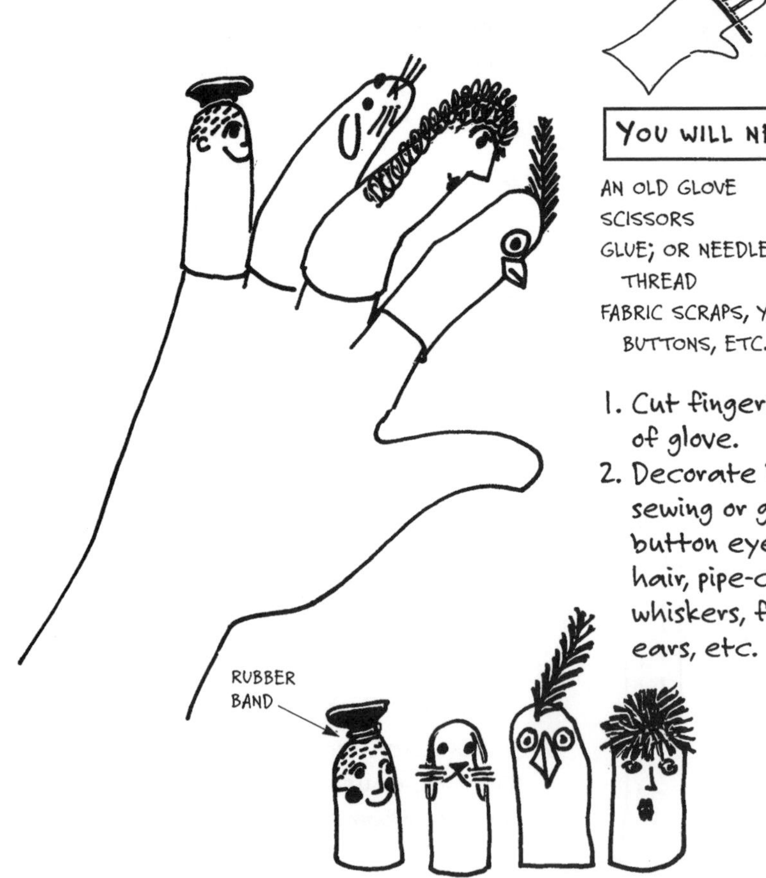

YOU WILL NEED:

AN OLD GLOVE
SCISSORS
GLUE; OR NEEDLE AND THREAD
FABRIC SCRAPS, YARN, BUTTONS, ETC.

1. Cut fingers off of glove.
2. Decorate by sewing or gluing on button eyes, yarn hair, pipe-cleaner whiskers, felt ears, etc.

ODD SOCK PUPPETS

Make a family of puppets.
Create some new characters
for the odd sock puppet theater!

YOU WILL NEED:

OLD SOCKS • GLUE; OR NEEDLE AND THREAD • FELT SCRAPS, RUG SCRAPS, YARN, BUTTONS, BEADS, RICKRACK, ETC.

Pull the sock over your hand and the heel over your thumb.

Make a fist, and talk with your fingers.

SOAP MITTEN

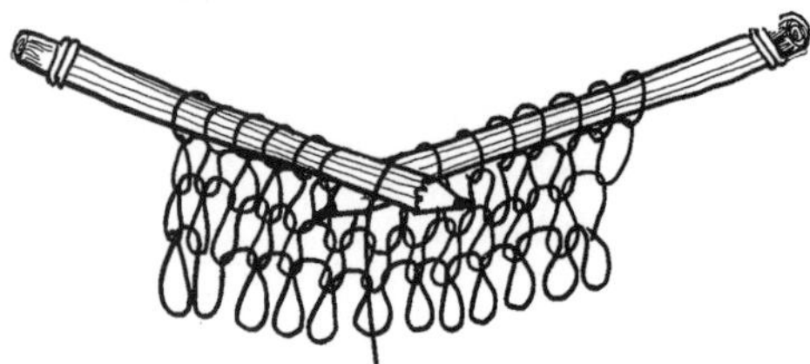

YOU WILL NEED:

2 NEW PENCILS
BALL OF COTTON TWINE OR KITE STRING
SCISSORS

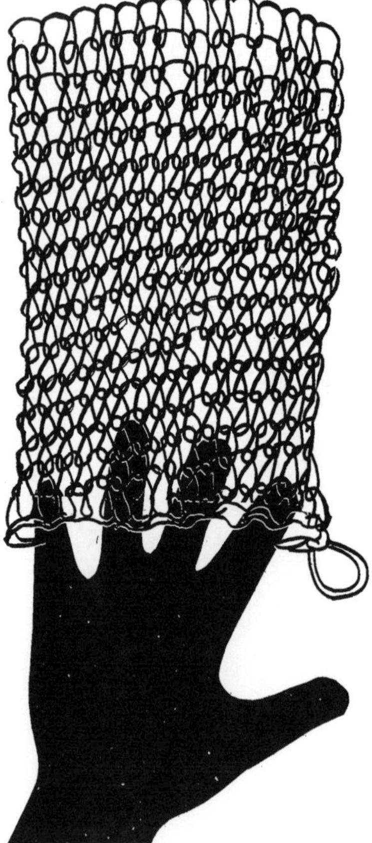

1. Using the pencils as knitting needles, cast on 26 stitches.
2. Knit 26 rows backward and forward.
3. Cast off loosely.
4. Fold square in half.
5. Sew the top and side together.
6. Get a cake of soap.
7. Put soap in mitten, and scrub your knees.

VOILÀ!

If you don't know how to knit, ask someone to teach you.

IVORY SOAP BOAT

YOU WILL NEED:

BAR OF IVORY SOAP
PENCIL
HEAVY PAPER
A BATHTUB OR POND

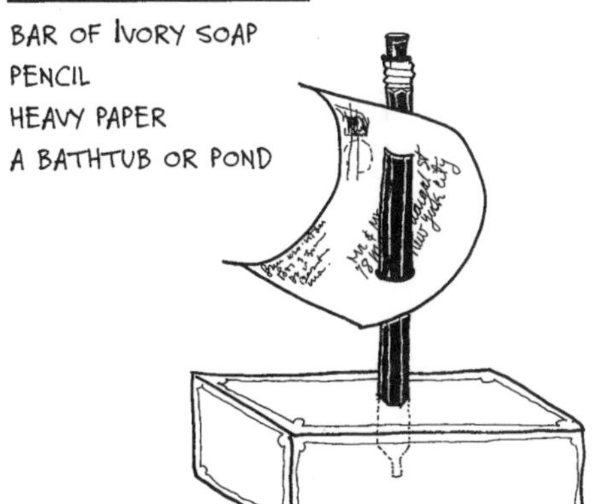

Ivory soap floats!

1. Poke pencil through a square of paper.
2. Poke pencil into soap.
3. Float soap boat in tub, and blow into the sail.

SOAP SCULPTURE

YOU WILL NEED:

BAR OF SOAP
PENCIL
KNIFE
NAIL OR PIN

You can carve soap with a kitchen knife. Draw a figure on the soap, and cut away the excess. Shape the edges, and smooth them with water. Decorate by drawing with nail or pin.

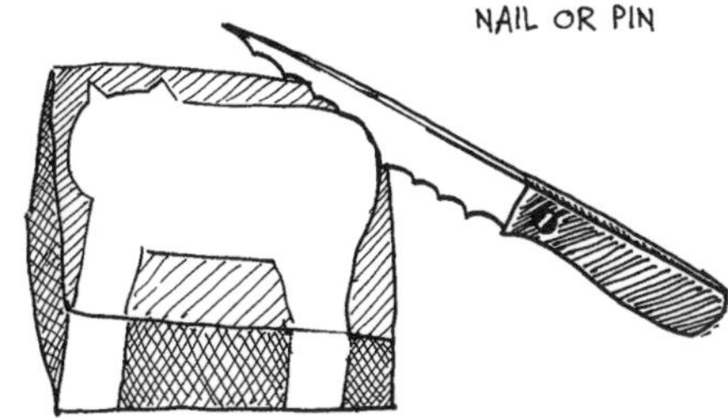

GIANT BUBBLES

YOU WILL NEED:

DISHPAN OR COOKIE SHEET • WATER • DISH DETERGENT (JOY DETERGENT WORKS WELL.) • WIRE COAT HANGERS • JUICE CANS • TAPE

Fill the dishpan or cookie sheet with warm water and a good splash of detergent.

Small bubble pipes can be made out of coat hangers or soda or juice cans with one

end off and a hole in the other end; dip the open end in the soap bath.

Tape 3 cans together.

Blow a dome on a cookie sheet.

But best of all and biggest . . . are bubbles made with glycerine and soap on a plastic-straw-and-string frame, a wonderful discovery enlarged at the Boston Children's Museum to delight little and big bubble lovers.

GIANT BUBBLE FRAME

Have an outdoor Giant Bubble Launching Contest.

YOU WILL NEED:

2 PLASTIC DRINKING STRAWS • STRING • GLYCERINE (GIVES THE SOAP FILM MORE ELASTICITY AND IRIDESCENCE; YOU CAN BUY A JAR AT THE DRUGSTORE.)

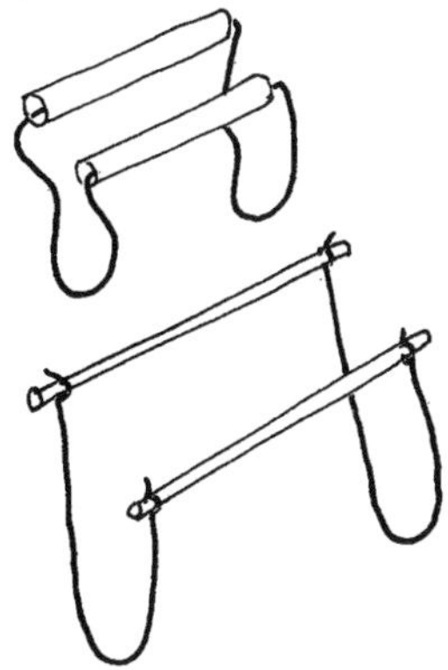

1. Thread 1 yard of string through 2 plastic straws. Knot string ends.

2. Add a dollop of glycerine to your pan of soapy water, and drop this contraption in.

3. Holding the straws, gather a film across the strings. Pull the straws apart to stretch the film open.
4. Pull upward, gently filling the film with air.
5. Relax the contraption, and snap the bubble free of the frame. Fantastic giant glistening rainbow bubbles will wobble into perfect globes.

GO FISH

YOU WILL NEED:

CRAYONS OR MARKERS
PAPER
SCISSORS
PAPER CLIPS
SMALL MAGNET
STRING
STICK

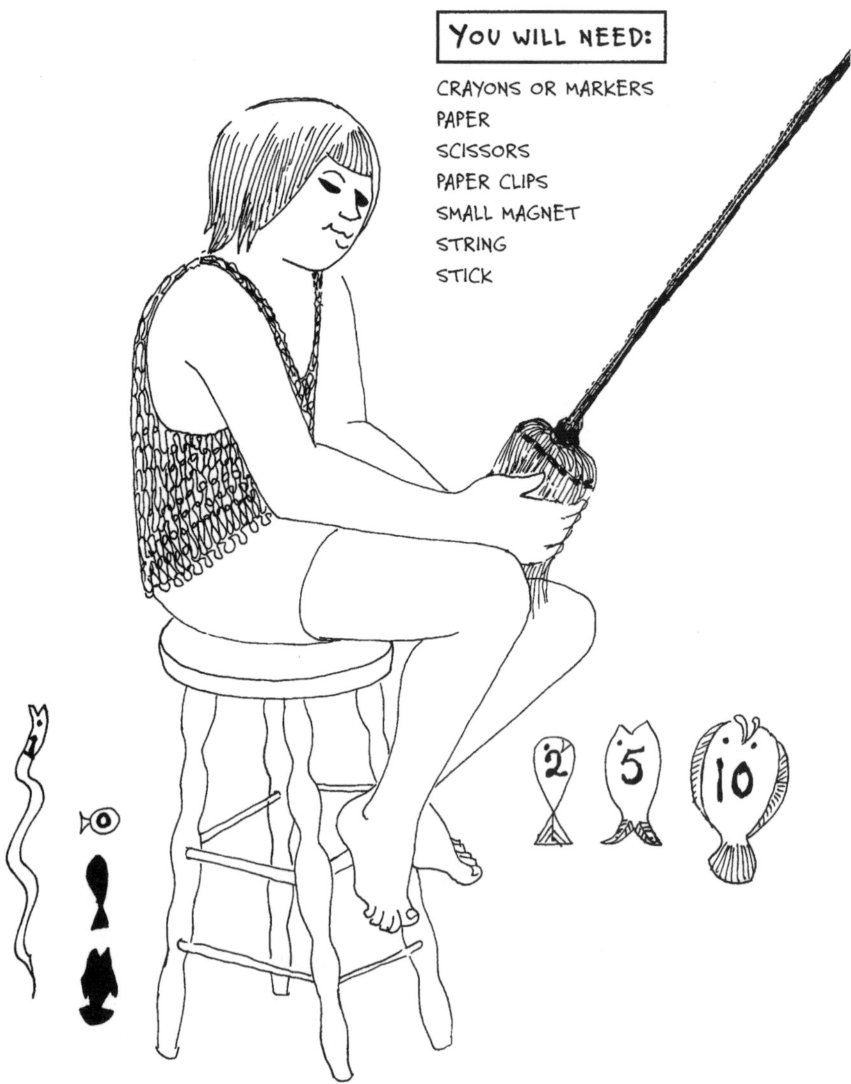

1. Draw a collection of little fish.
2. Give each fish a value.
3. Cut them out.
4. Put a paper clip on each one.
5. Tie the magnet to a string.
6. Tie the string to the stick.
7. Go fishing.

Make it into a game.
Fish for the answers to your arithmetic problems.

(If you can't find paper clips, try safety pins, straight pins, or tin-can lids, or weave bits of wire into fish.)

XYLOPHONE

YOU WILL NEED: $\frac{7}{8}$"- or $\frac{3}{4}$"-diameter copper or steel electrician's pipe (available at hardware store or lumber yard) • hacksaw or pipe cutter • 2 strips of rubber or fabric • glue • 2 strips of wood • pencil or dowel • rubber band

1. Cut pipe lengths with hacksaw or pipe cutter using the proportions shown.
2. Glue rubber or fabric to 2 strips of wood, and lay pipes across wood strips. OR just lay them across 2 belts.
3. A pencil with a rubber band wrapper around the eraser end (or a dowel with a rubber band around one end) makes a good hammer.

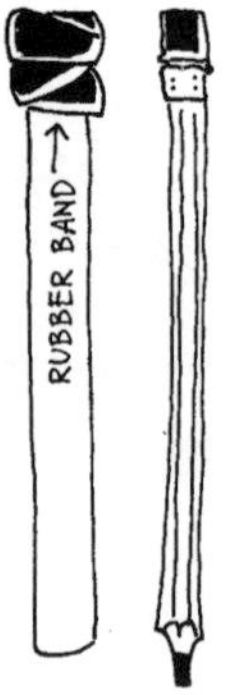

RUBBER BAND

Good xylophones are expensive, but you shall have music!

SWEET SOUNDS FROM FOUND OBJECTS

FROM THE KITCHEN AND THE JUNK HEAP

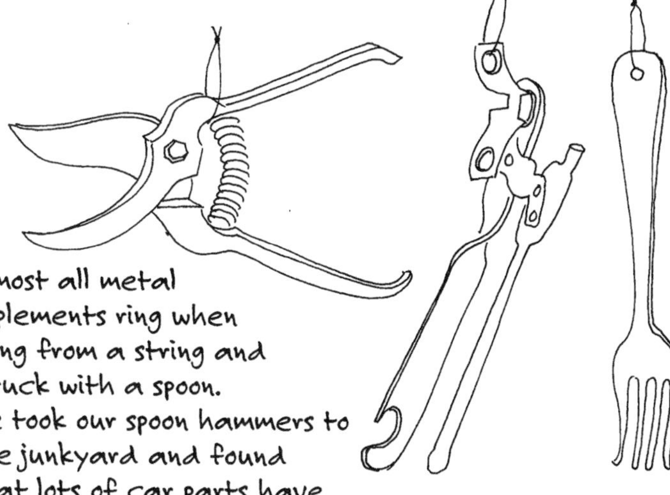

Almost all metal
implements ring when
hung from a string and
struck with a spoon.
We took our spoon hammers to
the junkyard and found
that lots of car parts have
bell-like sounds.
Collect a bunch of sounds.
Drill holes so you can hang them by strings.
Play them like timpani.
Play hubcap, car-part, gear-wheel cacophony!

DON'T JUST BANG — SYNCOPATE!

CANDLE CASTING

IN WET SAND

YOU WILL NEED:

SHOE BOX • SAND • PARAFFIN • CRAYONS • DOUBLE BOILER • HOT PLATE OR STOVE • TOOTHPICK • WICK STRING • SCISSORS

1. Fill shoe box with sand.
2. Add enough water to dampen sand.
3. Scoop out a hole, or screw your fist in the wet sand.
4. Poke thumb and 2 fingers into hole, down far enough to make leg molds.
5. Melt paraffin in double boiler. Melt crayon bits for color.
6. Pour melted wax into mold.
7. While wax is soft, make wick hole with toothpick.
8. Insert wick into candle. Pour in a tiny bit more warm wax to set wick.
9. When wax is cool, remove candle from sand.

Make mold with fist and fingers.
Cut wick.

Try different shapes.

Master Notes

- The sand sticks to the outside of the candle.
- If you want a thicker coat of sand, mix a canful of sand and wax together. Coat the hole with a thick wall of this mix. Then pour pure wax into center burning area.
- The wick can be introduced at pouring stage by tying a section of wick to a stick and resting it over the wax hole. Pour slowly so wick stands straight.
- Add candle hardener for better, longer-burning candles: $\frac{1}{2}$ pound stearic acid per 11-pound block of paraffin.
- Caution: Paraffin is dangerous. Never let it boil or overheat, only melt. Wax can ignite and smoke terribly. Always use double boiler. Warm wax makes a better candle than hot wax does. Wax fires must be smothered. Remove smoking wax outdoors.

CANDLE DIPPING

YOU WILL NEED:

2 COFFEE CANS • HOT PLATE OR STOVE • SOUP POT • PARAFFIN • WICK STRING • SCISSORS • CRAYONS

1. Fill one coffee can with cold water.
2. Fill second can 3/4 full of water. Place can in soup pot partially filled with water (to act as a double boiler). Heat.
3. Put paraffin slab into heating water. Allow wax to melt.
4. Prepare wick: Cut twice the depth of the can, about 12" for a tall candle, 6" for a short candle.
5. Hold wick in the center, and dip ends into hot wax and then into cold water, pulling wick straight. Go back and forth until your candle has grown to the size you like.
6. Cut your 2 candles apart, and have dinner by candlelight.

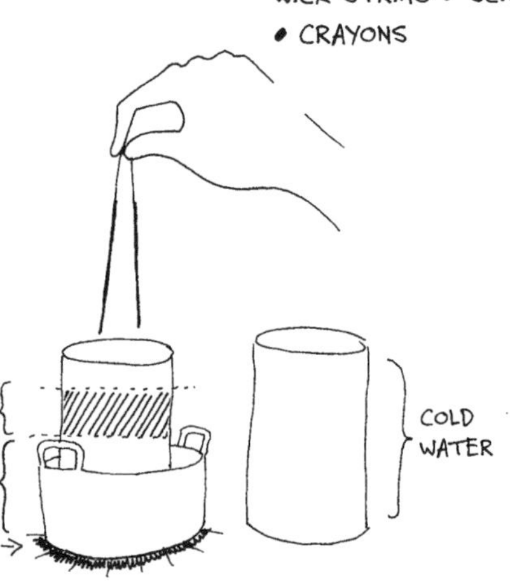

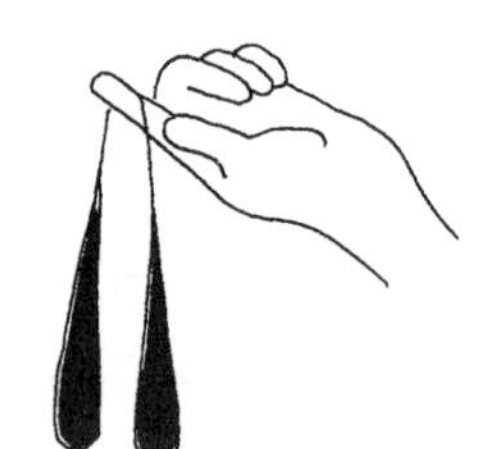

Remember, candles were early people's first fire keepers and night-lights. The candle — wick in wax — enabled people to extend their workday and see in the dark!

ENERGY TOYS

YOU WILL NEED:

BLOCK OF WOOD • SAW • HAMMER AND NAILS • RUBBER BANDS • TONGUE DEPRESSOR OR FLAT BIT OF WOOD • SPOOL • LOLLIPOP STICK OR THIN DOWEL • SLICE OF CANDLE • STRING • PLASTIC BOTTLE • PAPER CLIP • PAPER

PROPELLER BOAT

Cut boat out of wood. Hammer in 2 nails as shown. Attach rubber band to nails. Slip tongue depressor or bit of wood into rubber band. Twist. Put boat in water, and let go!

Also try cutting out a paper boat. Put a drop of oil or soap in circle.

Watch it go.

PLASTIC BOTTLE CAROUSEL

SPOOL CAROUSEL

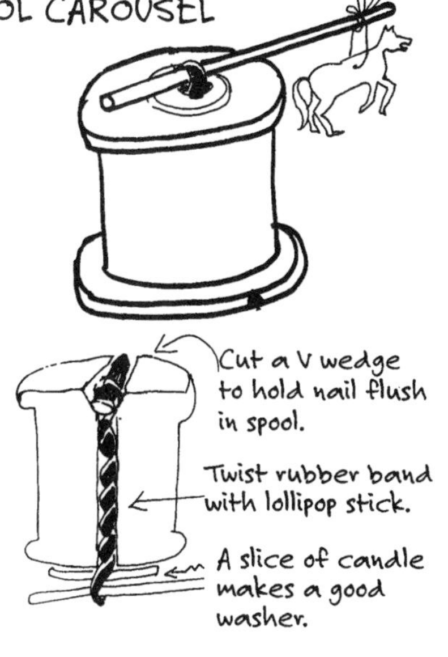
Cut a V wedge to hold nail flush in spool.
Twist rubber band with lollipop stick.
A slice of candle makes a good washer.

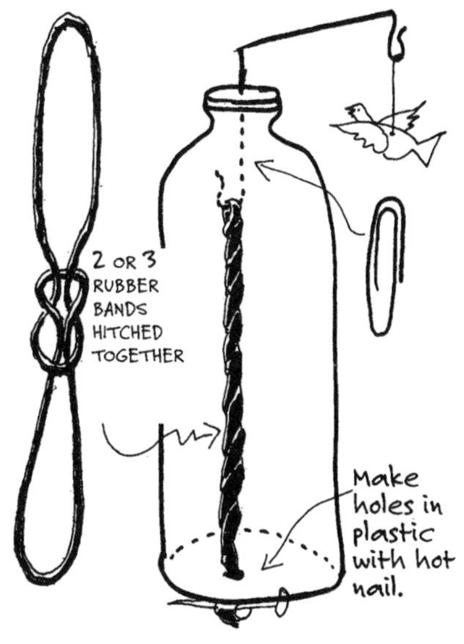
2 OR 3 RUBBER BANDS HITCHED TOGETHER
Make holes in plastic with hot nail.

BOX COSTUMES

YOU WILL NEED:

CORRUGATED CARDBOARD BOX BIG ENOUGH TO CLIMB INTO
SCISSORS
CRAYONS OR MARKERS
GLUE
2 BELTS OR STRIPS OF CLOTH
2 STICKS OR DOWELS

1. Cut flaps off box, and cut a hole to fit you.
2. Draw an animal, and cut it out. Glue on tail, trunk, etc.

3. Poke holes for shoulder straps, and adjust straps to fit you.
4. Tie straps around a stick inside box, so they don't pull through holes.

Good for plays, parades, and Halloween

BOX SCULPTURES

YOU WILL NEED:

MILK CARTONS • SHOE BOXES • EGG CARTONS • PAPER TOWEL TUBES AND TOILET PAPER TUBES • SCISSORS • GLUE OR TAPE • CRAYONS OR MARKERS • CONSTRUCTION PAPER • CLOTHESPINS

MILK CARTON HORSE

MILK CARTON CATAMARAN

SHOE BOX RABBIT

EGG CARTON CATERPILLAR

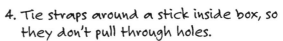

MILK CARTON BIRD

TOILET PAPER TUBE BIRD

WINDOW SHADE MAPS & MURALS

YOU WILL NEED:

OLD OR NEW PAPER WINDOW SHADES (AVAILABLE AT HARDWARE STORES)
CRAYONS, MARKERS, OR PAINT

Draw or paint:
a new horizon
a sunny garden
a summer dream
a window view
a design
a map

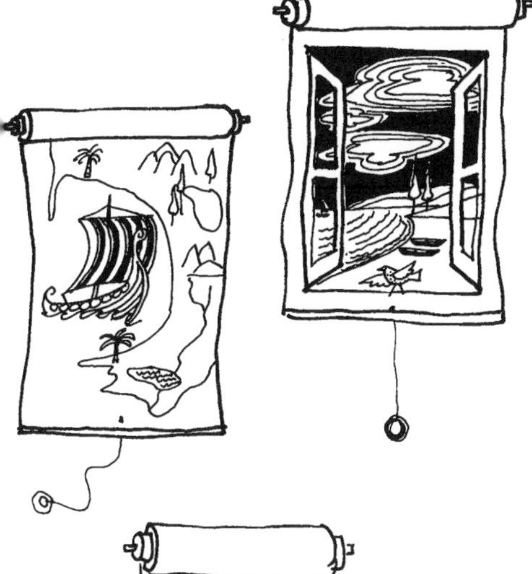

Hang them in windows or where you wish there were windows.

CRUSHED CANDY PEACE-AND-LOVE COOKIES

1. Use a plain cookie mix or this basic recipe:
   - $\frac{1}{3}$ cup vegetable shortening
   - $\frac{1}{3}$ cup sugar
   - 1 egg
   - 3 cups sifted all-purpose flour
   - $\frac{1}{2}$ tsp. baking soda, sifted with flour
   - 1 tsp. salt, scant
   - $\frac{2}{3}$ cup honey
2. Roll chilled dough into sausage strips about $\frac{1}{4}$" thick for strong outlines. Be sure pieces connect for strength.
3. Make designs on aluminum foil over a cookie sheet.
4. <u>Colored filling</u>: Crack up lollipops or hard candy. Sprinkle in openings.
5. <u>Bake</u> at 375° about 8 to 10 minutes.

Note:
Don't make a stained glass sculpture bigger than your oven!

6. Sticks: Cookies can be baked with or without sticks. Sticks can be baked in place if your oven is big enough. OR press stick into cookie while it is still warm and soft. Use $\frac{1}{8}$" or $\frac{1}{4}$" wooden dowels.
7. Cool. When dough is firm, peel off aluminum foil.

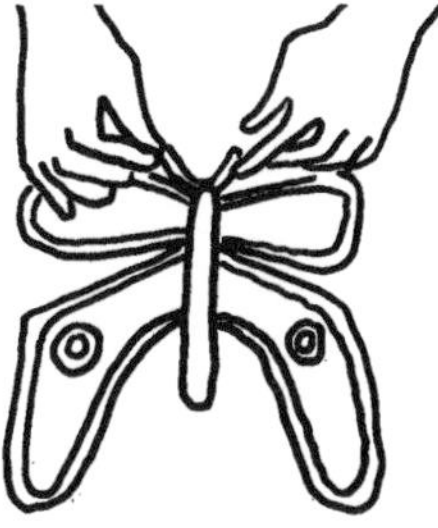

Ilse invented this cookie innovation — what a beautiful discovery! Ilse and Philip Johnston, both artists, have wonderful bake-ins and invite neighbors and friends to discover their own talents.

EDIBLE

BREAD DOUGH SCULPTURES

Bread: the staff of life and the bond of friendship. To break it is to share. To make it is to care.

BASIC BREAD RECIPE

1 PACKAGE YEAST • 2 CUPS WARM WATER • 3 TBLSP. SUGAR OR HONEY • 2 TSP. SALT • $\frac{1}{4}$ CUP OIL • 7 CUPS FLOUR

Start yeast in warm sugar water. Let it stand 5 minutes to start yeast working. Add salt, oil, and flour, a little at a time until you can work dough with your hands. If dough is sticky, add more flour. Knead, and make sculpture on cookie sheet or aluminum foil.

Dough sculpture must lie flat, not standing. Make pancake, snakes, and ball shapes. Stick them together with a little water, or lick your finger. The wet parts will grow together as the dough rises. Let rise 10 to 20 minutes. Bake at 350° for 20 to 30 minutes, depending on size of figure.

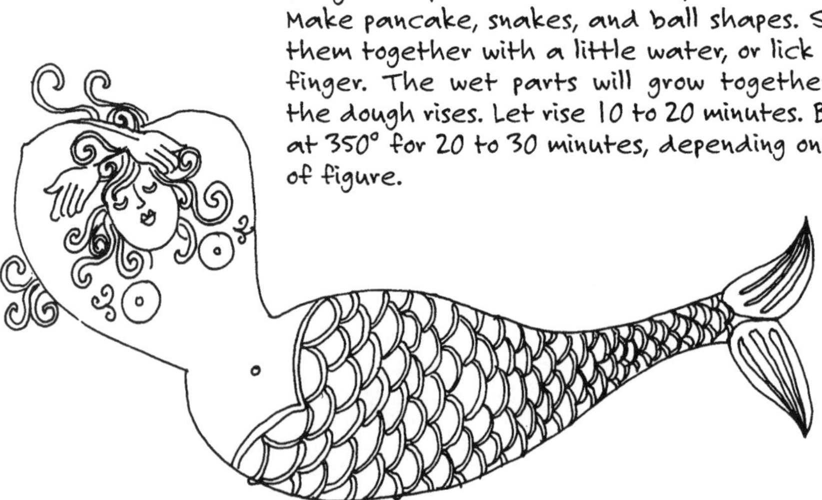

To celebrate the opening of the "Art, Food, and Technology" exhibit at the Institute of Contemporary Art in Boston, Drago's Bakery and I made a 5-foot-long, 25-pound bread mermaid. She was eaten at midnight in 20 minutes. Yum.

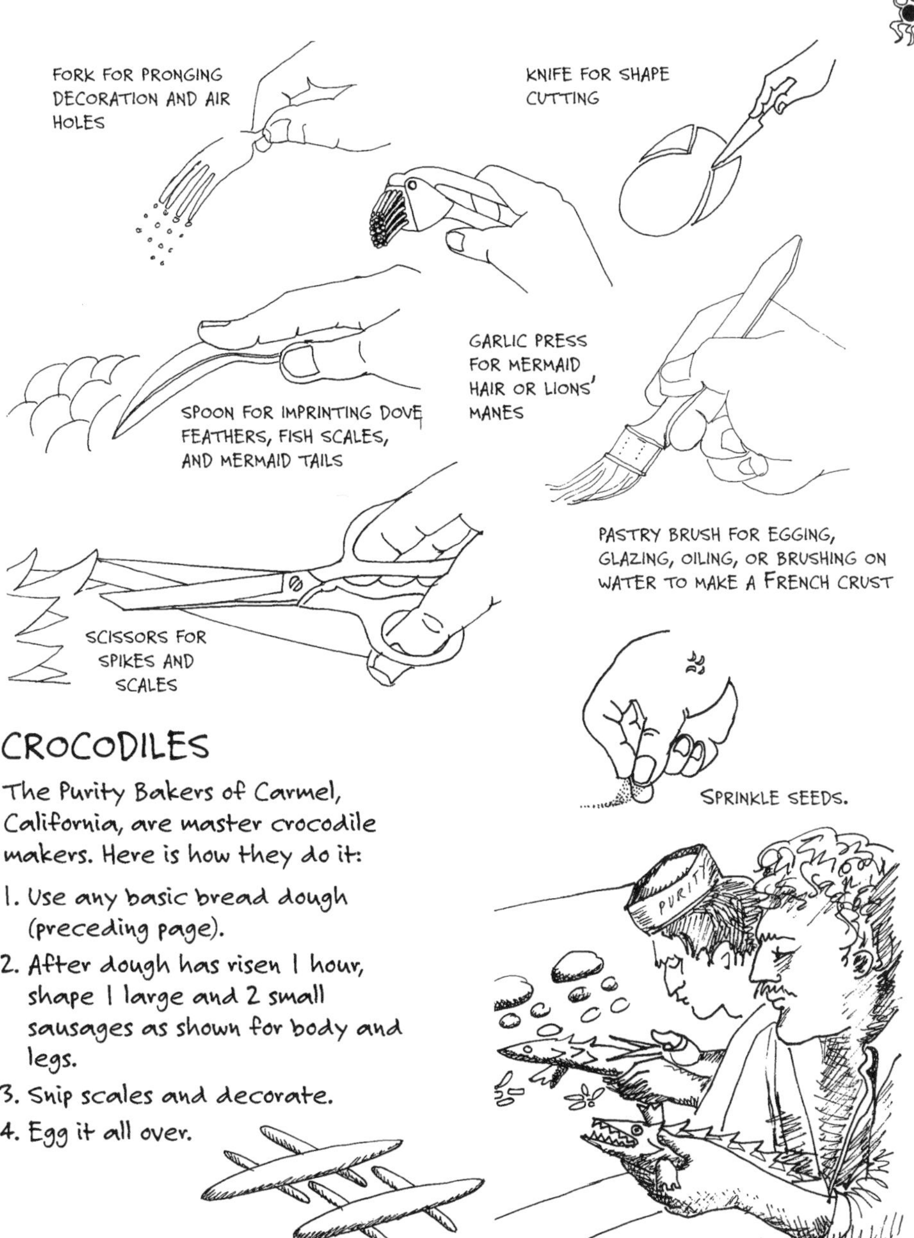

CROCODILES

The Purity Bakers of Carmel, California, are master crocodile makers. Here is how they do it:

1. Use any basic bread dough (preceding page).
2. After dough has risen 1 hour, shape 1 large and 2 small sausages as shown for body and legs.
3. Snip scales and decorate.
4. Egg it all over.

PEACEABLE BREAD

For important festivals and special friends. Use any light bread recipe, or see page 140. Prepare dough not too dry, not too sticky.

Using a commercial oven, the biggest Peaceable Bread we ever baked was 27 pounds (4'x 3') for LIFE magazine's Christmas issue, 1972.

Cut toes.
Stick all sections together with a dab of water. And don't make a sculpture bigger than your oven!

1. Divide dough into 1 big ball and 6 medium balls.
2. Flatten the big ball into a rectangle for body. Place it as shown on cookie sheet or oven shelf covered with foil.

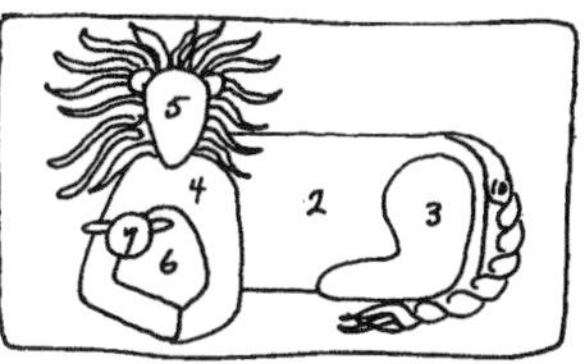

3. Form #3 shape for back leg out of one of the medium dough balls.
4. Flatten another ball and form #4 arms.
5. Form #5 piece for head of lion.
6. Form a bun shape for lamb's body #6. Tuck it in lion's arms.
7. Make a small ball for lamb's head #7. Add ears.
8. Cut or form the 2 noses from a flattened piece of dough. (Use a dab of water as glue.)
9. Roll all the rest of the dough into snakes for the mane and lamb's curls.
10. Save 3 long snakes for the braided or twisted lion's tail #10.
11. Use raisins for eyes.
12. Poke fork prongs into body of lion as air holes (so he won't split open) and decoration.
13. Whip up a raw egg, and gently paint your beasts all over.
14. Let rise 10 minutes and bake at 350° about 45 minutes, depending on size. EAT. . . .

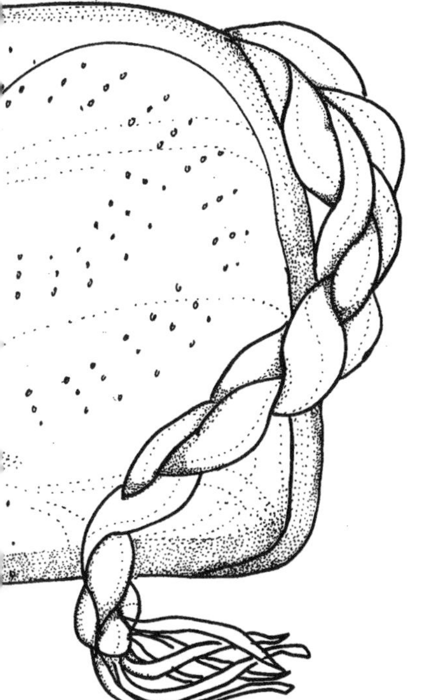

CASTING PLASTER

Plaster of paris is temperamental.
It sets quickly.
It dries fast,
but it stays soggy
if the air is damp
or if the proportions are wrong.
It scratches easily;
it breaks easily if dropped.
But it is easy to use:
good for building up sculptures,
quick casting, and
plaster scrimshaw
pendants and rubbings.
Plaster blocks are also good for carving.

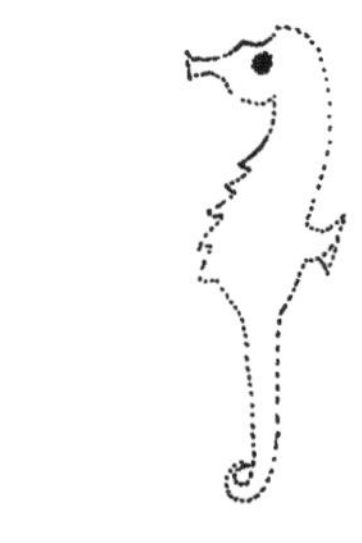

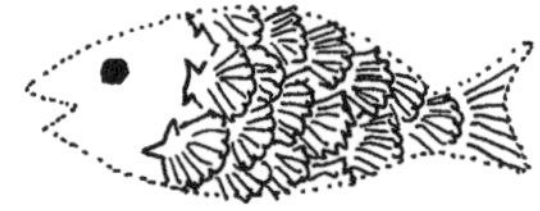

THE HAND PLAQUE

YOU WILL NEED:

PLASTER OF PARIS
PIE TIN
OIL OR VASELINE

No matter how over-worked the idea, it's pretty sweet to have that little hand printed in plaster. Pour plaster of paris into a small oiled pie dish. Press hand into plaster mix; hold it just a moment or two until plaster sets.

Mommies love this!

SAND CASTING

YOU WILL NEED:

SHOE BOX • SAND • STICK • FORK, SPOON • SHELLS, SEA GLASS, ETC. • PLASTIC BOWL • 5 POUNDS PLASTER OF PARIS • PAPER CLIP

WITH PLASTER OF PARIS
(For sunny, dry days only)

If you can do this on the beach, the sea will wash away the mess. An outdoor sand pile works well, too, but a shoe box full of sand will do.

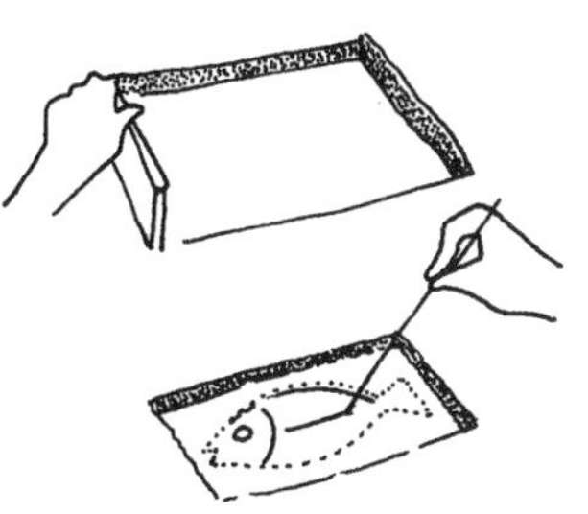

1. Partially fill shoe box with wet sand. OR make a smooth 1"-deep ditch in wet sand (in sandbox or at the beach) with your hand or a shingle.
2. Draw your picture with a stick.
3. Decorate with fork or spoon marks, shell imprints, colored sea glass, beach pebbles, etc.

4. Mix plaster, enough to fill the area: Pour water in bowl. Pour plaster powder into water until mountain peak rises above water level. Stir until smooth and as thick as frosting.
5. Quickly pour mixture on top of drawing about 1" or 2" thick.
6. Stick a paper clip in the middle of the top edge of your figure to act as a hanger.
7. Allow plaster to set about 10 minutes or until no longer warm.
8. Lift plaster cast out of sand. Brush it off, and hang it up at home.

YOU WILL NEED: PLASTER OF PARIS • WATER • BOWL • WAX PAPER • SPOON • PAPER CLIP, NAIL, OR PIN • STRING OR THONG (OPTIONAL)

PLASTER SCRIMSHAW

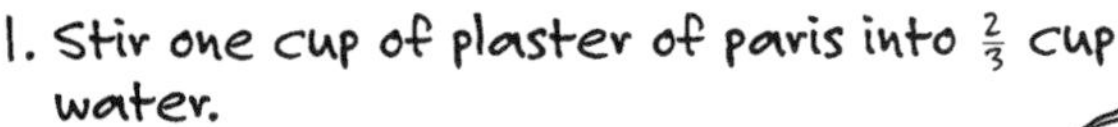

1. Stir one cup of plaster of paris into $\frac{2}{3}$ cup water.
2. Mix until thick and smooth. (Use quickly; it hardens fast!)

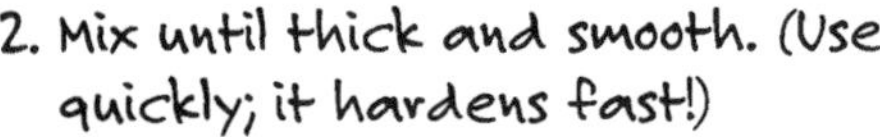

3. Drop spoonfuls like cookies onto wax paper. Insert paper clip hanger, or use nail to poke hole for string.
4. Allow 5 to 10 minutes to harden.
5. Use paper clip, nail, or pin to etch a design. You can scratch it, paint it, shellac it, put a leather thong through it and wear it . . . Or you can make rubbings from it: Put a sheet of paper on top of your design, and rub a flat crayon over it.

SOUP BONE SCRIMSHAW

When we lived in Florence, the butcher gave us lots of bones for soup. When the bones were boiled clean, my boys made napkin rings with scratched designs. Rub ink into the scratches so design will stand out better.

PLASTER CARVING BLOCKS

YOU WILL NEED: PLASTER OF PARIS • BOWL • MILK CARTON OR SHOE BOX • KNIFE OR SCULPTING TOOLS

1. Pour mixed plaster of paris into a milk carton or shoe box, depending on how big a carving block you want.
2. When plaster is set (no longer warm), tear off box.
3. Carve block with kitchen tools or sculpture chisels.

Master Notes

- Dipping plaster block in water makes carving easier.
- Salt in the plaster mix speeds thickening (that's why using the ocean works so well).
- Oil or Vaseline protects against plaster sticking to mold.
- Vinegar retards drying.
- Coffee grounds or vermiculite added to plaster mix makes interesting textures for sculpture.
- Wet plaster can also be used to build up form on an armature, then filed or sanded to perfection.
- Plastic bowls or buckets are best — rinse immediately.
- Caution: Plaster clogs sink drains! Dump it outside.

In the question lies the answer.

The how is in the doing.

In the process . . . is the discovery.

Evolving from within . . . growing out of real needs.

CONNECTING THINGS WITH IDEAS

Things to Discover Through Bookmaking

Record keeping, documentation, the recording of history, keeping a journal, fact collecting, chemistry of inks and fibers, sewing and gluing, problem solving, book binding, other languages, laws, idea clarification, mass distribution of information, sharing of experience, preservation of traditional artisanry, self-expression, poetry, calligraphy, typography, engraving, printing, paper making, and the mathematics of signatures.

Things to Discover Through Paper Making

The fabric of fibers, plants, and vegetables; making slurry; recycling waste paper; water suspension; drying; pressing; colors and dyes. The many uses of paper: for communication, advertising, announcements, wrapping, containers, writing, drawing, insulation, and construction.

Things to Discover Through the Fiber Arts

The making of fabrics; animals that taught us to weave and mesh grasses and twigs; the making of containers for carrying, storing food, and catching fish; fibers for building, body covering, shelter, suspension, and protection from danger, from insects, and from animals; sieving, sinking, dragging, burying, juicing, joining, tying together, lashing, stabilizing, mooring, holding, leading, lacing, spinning, pattern making, stitching, rope making, sewing, bedding, rug making, ancient history, and anthropology.

Things to Discover Through Game Making

Problem solving, rule following, mathematics of scoring, counting, memory retention, teamsmanship, group cooperation and involvement, invention, thinking, creating strategies, winning vs. losing, speculation, risking, bluffing, patience.

QUESTIONS

"What'll I Do?"

Usually said by children; freely translated, means "What can I do that won't be dirty, make a mess, waste materials, get in your way, or require me to wait?" (Remember that waiting is real punishment for a young child full of excited curiosity and instant appetites, hoping for instant gratification.)

"Will You Show Me How?"

Means "Please stop, go slowly, and make it clear so I, too, can own this skill and do it well, all by myself!" Also means "Don't do it for me but hang in while I learn."

"Is This Right?"

Means "Is it as good as yours?" or "Do I have permission to experiment, and will you give me approval even if it isn't just like yours?"

"Thank You for Showing Me" and "I Can Do It"

Mean "You have given me the gift of myself — I needed help finding out if I could do it; I needed help finding me."

SOLUTIONS

Needed:

An enlarged, expansive attitude toward space. Tolerance for mishap or arrangements to accommodate it. Every work produces waste. Incorporate the idea; anticipate the inevitable.

Stop:

Simplify; explain the logic. It helps understanding and heightens interest. It's easy if child independence is truly your goal.

Right by Whose Standards?

What is right? The right that makes things work, please, or improve. Give permission to experiment — <u>that</u> is right. Many new materials and ideas came out of mistakes and things not right. Encourage the things that are rather than dwelling on the things that aren't.

Provide Ways to:

Develop independence, self-reliance, pride of accomplishment, and self-expression — a good self-image.

THE MAKING OF MAKING THINGS

This book grew out of my need to explain process to large groups of students. I've always loved raw materials and thinking up creative ways to use them. Here are some of the projects I cooked up during the years leading up to and around the first MAKING THINGS books. You can re-create them at home, at school, at parties, at camp, or at fairs to earn your own way.

Sand Fountains

In the late 1950s and early 1960s, when my two boys were little, we lived in Maine and for three years in Italy. We were living close to the bone and were always making things like bread sculpture, hooked rugs, furniture, moccasins, stilts, books, hammocks, jewelry, belts, and bags.

In 1963, we returned to the United States and moved to Princeton, New Jersey. During this time, I was exhibiting my paintings, teaching crafts, and making tapestry commissions. I invented the "Sand Fountain," a rotating glass box through which sand spilled and objects moved. I sold fifty of them when someone brought them to the attention of David Rockefeller, who bought five for the Chase Manhattan Bank Art Collection, and Joseph Hirschhorn, who bought the remainder of my collection just as we were moving to Boston.

Stuart School Hooked Tapestry

I proposed a tapestry program for the Stuart Country Day School, in Princeton, where I later became art director. The whole student body was involved in the making of two twelve-foot hooked tapestries. The one shown here is "The Epic of Gilgamesh." The first tapestry was called "In the Beginning." It was such a splendid work of art that the Metropolitan Museum, in New York City, asked to hang it in their library.

New York Tapestry

In 1967, the Metropolitan Museum sponsored a tapestry program I conducted for a group composed of children from Harlem and children of museum members. We spent twenty-five Saturdays making this twelve-foot tapestry called "New York, New York, We Beautified New York," which hung in the museum for many years. The International Film Foundation documented this project, and the film was shown from time to time in the museum theater.

The Paper-Making Factory

While I was program director for the visitors center of the Boston Children's Museum (while it was in Jamaica Plain), we ran a kitchen-style paper-making factory. Every visitor could make a sheet of paper from scratch — tear the pulp, blend the mash, deckle the slurry, iron the wet leaf — and then potato-print a design on it. The idea spread all over the country. Now artists have made it into a fine art.

Summerthing D Street Mural

Boston's Summerthing program hired a group of artists to supervise the creation of a block-long mural on the wooden wall that surrounded the burned remains from the terrible Coconut Grove fire on D Street and Broadway. Adults, children, and passers-by painted all weekend.

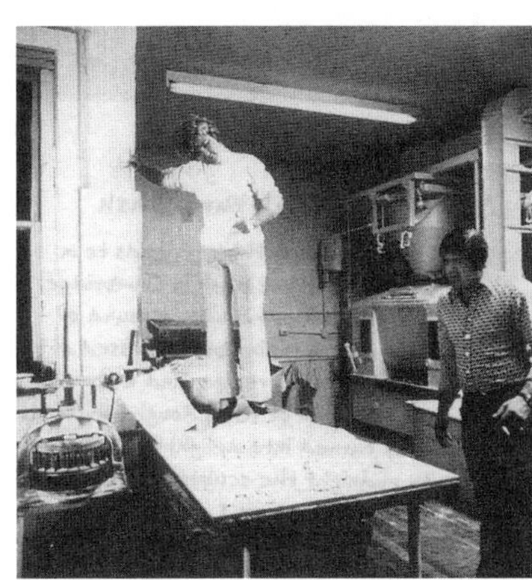

The Christmas Peaceable Bread

In 1972, LIFE magazine came to Boston to photograph my giant Christmas Bread sculpture of the lion and lamb (see page 142) for a special holiday issue called "Joys of Christmas." This thirty-pound Peaceable Bread was baked in the big oven of a Boston bakery and eaten by the students at the Commonwealth School.

New Hampshire Teachers Creativity Enrichment Program

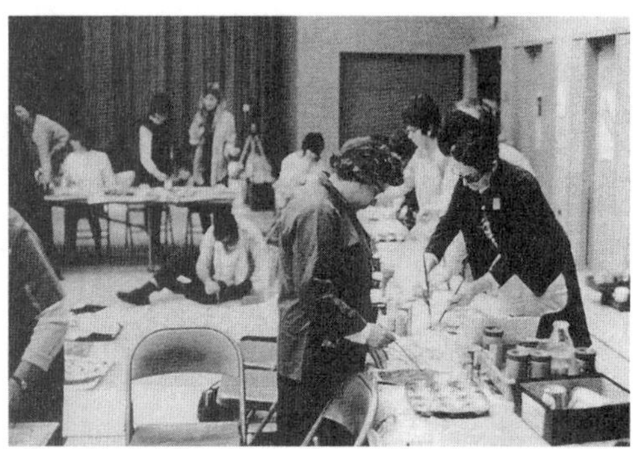

The New Hampshire Commission on the Arts sponsored twenty-five creativity enrichment workshops for southern New Hampshire elementary school teachers. I worked with as many as ninety teachers on Friday afternoons in a big gymnasium with tables full of projects and materials. Everybody made one of everything and took the ideas and recipes back to their schools. The projects included how to teach math through weaving, history through paper making, and science through balancing toys. That was the start of MAKING THINGS.

Boston Bicentennial Appliquéd Cloth Mural

In preparation for the Boston Bicentennial, the mayor's cultural program hired eight artists to work with groups of senior citizens around the Boston area. My group was in Allston-Brighton. We had about twenty-five women, many of whom were immigrants who knew how to embroider. They created a seventy-two-foot appliquéd tapestry depicting American Independence, one of eight tapestries that hung in City Hall for the bicentennial year. The women signed the work by creating one-foot-square self-portraits stitched in the San Blas method, which were sewn, like little flags, along the bottom of our tapestry.

Bread Sculpture Bash

I invited about thirty friends to a bread sculpture bash in Cambridge. Each person came with a pound of flour and a mixing bowl. I passed out a basic bread recipe, and everyone made a ball of rising dough, which they turned into delightful sculptures. By midnight the sculptures were all glazed, baked, and on exhibit. At midnight we ate them warm with butter and jam.

BU Students Creating with Marsh Fibers

I took a class of Boston University students down to the marshes at Scituate and challenged them to create structures, shelters, body coverings, and baskets out of nature's available materials. By the end of the day, they had woven, bound, wrapped, and constructed driftwood looms, straw baskets, reed sun hats, thong sandals, and a hut made out of weeds and sticks.

The Thousand Balancing Clothespin Circus

The winter I lived in Provincetown, overlooking the bay, the marine specialty store was selling bags of wooden clothespin rejects. I couldn't resist the shape — they looked like little people. Adding pipe cleaners for arms, I turned them into acrobats, dancers, and balancing toys. My circus grew to thousands of clothespin performers with fifty imaginary animals made out of wood scraps from the waste bin at my carpentry class. The following year, the DeCordova Museum, in Lincoln, announced their exhibit "Toys Made by Artists," where my Thousand Balancing Clothespin Circus of Endangered Species had its debut. When that show closed, the circus moved to the Montshire Science Museum, in Norwich, Vermont, where I ran a balancing toy workshop, after which one of the schools in town was inspired to create their own circus.

ART AND CRAFT BOOKS

Atwater, Mary M. **Byways in Handweaving.** Coupeville, Wash.: Shuttle Craft, 1988.

Baker, Arthur. **Calligraphy.** New York: Dover, 1973.

Biegeleisen, Jacob I. **Complete Book of Silk Screen Printing Production.** New York: Dover, 1963.

——— and J. A. Cohn. **Silk Screen Techniques.** New York: Dover, 1958.

Burnham, Dorothy K. **Cut My Cote.** Toronto: University of Toronto Press, 1994.

Burnham, Harold B. and Dorothy K. **Keep Me Warm One Night: Early Handweaving in Eastern Canada.** Toronto: University of Toronto Press, 1972.

Cannon, John and Margaret. **Dye Plants and Dyeing.** Portland, Or.: Timber, 1994.

Collingwood, Peter. **The Techniques of Rug Weaving.** New York: Watson-Guptill, 1987.

Ellenberger, W., et al. **Atlas of Animal Anatomy for Artists.** New York: Dover, 1956.

Gray, Henry. **Gray's Anatomy.** New York: Random House Value, 1977.

Hunt, Leslie. **Twenty-Five Kites that Fly.** New York: Dover, 1971.

Ickis, Marguerite. **The Standard Book of Quilt Making and Collecting.** New York: Dover, 1949.

Lanteri, Edouard. **Modelling and Sculpting Animals.** New York: Dover, 1985.

———. **Modelling and Sculpting the Human Figure.** New York: Dover, 1985.

Maryon, Herbert. **Metalwork and Enamelling.** 4th edition. New York: Dover, 1971.

Nelson, Glenn C. **Ceramics: A Potter's Handbook.** 5th edition. Fort Worth: Harcourt Brace College Publishers, 1984.

Regensteiner, Else. **The Art of Weaving.** Kadyville, N.Y.: Schiffer, 1986.

Untracht, Oppi. **Metal Techniques for Craftsmen.** New York: Doubleday, 1968.

Wachowiak, Frank, and Robert D. Clements. **Emphasis Art: A Qualitative Art Program for Elementary and Middle Schools.** 5th edition. New York: HarperCollins College, 1993.

Wagner, Willis H. **Modern Carpentry.** Revised edition. South Holland, Ill.: Goodheart, 1992.

———. **Modern Woodworking.** South Holland, Ill.: Goodheart, 1991.

BOOKS ON WAYS OF LEARNING

Ashton-Warner, Sylvia. **Teacher.** New York: Simon & Schuster, 1986.

Axline, Virginia M. **Dibs in Search of Self.** New York: Ballantine, 1986.

Cremin, Lawrence A. **The Transformation of the School: Progressivism in American Education, 1876–1957.** New York: McGraw-Hill, 1964.

Dennison, George. **The Lives of Children.** Reading, Mass.: Addison-Wesley, 1990.

Erikson, Erik H. **Childhood and Society.** New York: Norton, 1993.

Featherstone, Joseph. **Schools Where Children Learn.** New York: Liveright, 1971.

Fraiberg, Selma H. **The Magic Years: Understanding and Handling the Problems of Early Childhood.** New York: Macmillan, 1966.

Froebel, Friedrich. **Education of Man.** New York: Kelley, 1974.

Ginsburg, Herbert P., and Sylvia Opper. **Piaget's Theory of Intellectual Development.** 3rd edition. Englewood Cliffs, N.J.: Prentice-Hall, 1988.

Hawins, Frances P. **The Logic of Action: Young Children at Work.** Boulder: University of Colorado Press, 1986.

Holt, John. **How Children Fail.** Revised edition. New York: Dell, 1988.

Isaacs, Susan S. **Social Development in Young Children: A Study of Beginners.** New York: AMS Press, 1933.

Kohl, Herbert R. **Thirty-Six Children.** New York: NAL/Dutton, 1988.

Kozol, Jonathan. **Death at an Early Age.** New York: NAL/Dutton, 1985.

Leonard, George. **Education and Ecstasy: With the Great School Reform Hoax.** Revised edition. Berkeley, Calif.: North Atlantic, 1987.

Lowenfeld, Viktor, and W. Lambert Brittain. **Creative and Mental Growth.** 8th edition. New York: Macmillan, 1987.

Moffett, James, and Betty J. Wagner. **A Student-Centered Language Arts, K–12.** 4th edition. Portsmouth, N.H.: Boynton Cook, 1991.

Montessori, Maria. **Spontaneous Activity in Education.** Sage, Calif.: Education System Publishers, 1984.

Postman, Neil, and Charles Weingartner. **Teaching as a Subversive Activity.** New York: Dell, 1987.

Talbot, Toby. **The World of the Child: Clinical and Cultural Studies from Birth to Adolescence.** Northvale, N.J.: Aronson, 1974.

Toffler, Alvin. **Future Shock.** New York: Bantam, 1984.

Way, Brian. **Development Through Drama.** Highlands, N.J.: Humanities, 1967.

INDEX

animals: butterflies, 16, 42; costumes, 136; crocodiles, 141; horse, 72, 136; lion & lamb, 142–143; mouse, 64; sculptures, 136; slotted, 50; turtles, 73. See also birds; fish
appliqué, 65, 153

bailer, 79
balancing: shapes, 57; toys, 54–55
batik, 118–119
belts: macramé, 103; twisted yarn, 86–87; woven, 89, 91, 98
birds: balancing, 57; costumes, 136; feeder, 76; flapping owl, 11; Kiko's seagull, 10; paper cone, 5; box, 136
boats, 125, 135, 136
bookmaking, 36–43, 149
boxes: costumes, 136; horse, 72; houses, 70–71; looms, 88, 92–93; sculptures, 136
bread, 140–141, 142–143, 152
bubbles, 126–127

camping aids, 78–79
candles, 132–134
cardboard: balancing shapes, 57; birds, 10–11, 57; bookmaking, 36–43; cut-away, 24, 30; fold & cut, 12; marionettes, 48–49; mobiles, 56; racing turtles, 73; slotted animals, 50; zoetrope, 83. See also boxes

carousels, 135
casting: candles, 132–133; plaster, 144; sand, 145
clay leaves, 44
climbing pull toys, 51
cloth book jackets, 40–41
clothing: body-logic, 112–113; donut blouse, 114–115; grass, 80–81; quick, 110–111; vest, 108–109
cookies, 138–139
costumes, 110–112, 121, 136
crayon activities, 47

doll houses, 70–71
dolls, 62
dyeing, 116–119

energy toys, 135

feather balancer, 55
finger: paint, 46; printing, 25; puppets, 22, 122
fish: Go Fish, 128–129; mobiles, 16–17; printing, 33; scaler, 79; tissue, 17
fold & cut, 12
foot risers, 75
funnel, 79

games: Go Fish, 128–129
glider, 18
Go Fish game, 128–129
grass mats, 80–81, 153

hats, grass, 80–81
heddle looms, 90–93
helicopters, 19
houses, 70–71

jewelry, 14–15, 44–45, 53, 104

kites, 84–85
knitting, 108–109, 124
knots, 102, 106–107

looms, 88–99

macramé, 102–105
map keeper, 79
marionettes, 48–49
masks, 20–21, 120
mats, grass, 80–81
milk cartons, 54, 136
mobiles, 4, 16–17, 56, 58–59
movies, 82–83
musical instruments, 130–131

ornaments, 4, 45, 52

paint, finger, 46
pants hanger, 77
paper: bag puppets, 23; beads, 14–15; birds, 5, 10; boats, 135; bookmaking, 36–43; curls, 16; finger puppets, 22; fold & cut, 12; glider, 18; Go Fish, 128–129; lace hangers, 2–4; making, 6–9, 149, 155; marbleized, 34; masks, 20–21; mobiles, 4, 16–17; movies, 82–83; pendulum, 60–61; sculptures, 5; smoke, 35; spinners, 19; star balls, 4; 3-D scenes, 13; tissue fish, 17; towel dyeing, 116. See also cardboard

paper clip necklaces, 45
pasta necklaces, 45
pendulum, salt, 60–61
pillow cozies, 63
pinwheel, 19
plaster, 144–145, 146, 147
plastic bag kite, 85
plastic bottles: bailer/ funnel, 79; carousel, 135
Popsicle stick loom, 91
pouches: grass, 80–81; love, 105; mouse, 64; twining, 100–101
printing: block, 24, 30–31; fingers, 25; fish, 33; objects, 26; pudding, 46; roller, 32; vegetables, 26–29
puppets, 22–23, 48–49, 122–123

racing turtles, 73
rope winding, 87
rubbings, 47
rugs: hooking, 68–69; rag tail, 94–95

salt pendulum, 60–61
sand casting, 132–133, 145
scratchboards, 30, 47
scrimshaw, 146
sculptures: box, 136; bread, 140–143, 152; paper, 5; soap, 125
sewing: appliqué, 65, 153; bed friends & umm-dears, 62; clothing, 110–115; grass, 80–81; mouse pouch, 64; stitchery, 65–67
sharpener, 78
slotted animals, 50
soap: boats, 125; bubbles, 126–127; mitten, 124; sculpture, 125
soles, grass, 80–81
spools, 32, 135
stained glass: cookies, 138–139; crayon, 47
star balls, 4
stilts, 74–75
stitchery, 65–67
stocking masks & wigs, 120–121
straws: belt loom, 89; bubble frames, 127; mobile, 58–59
string/yarn: belts, 86–87, 89, 91; dispenser, 76; soap mitten, 124; twining, 100–101; twisting, 86–87
Styrofoam, 30, 50, 54

3-D stand-up scenes, 13
tie-dye, 116–117
tin cans: foot risers, 75; lid ornaments, 52; map keeper, 79; tripod, 78
twining, 100–101
twisting, 86–87

vegetable: fiber paper, 6–7; printing, 26–29

weaving, 88–101
weeds: dyes, 117; mats, 80–81, 153; weaving, 99, 153
wigs, braid, 121
window shades, 137
wire: hangers, 76–77, 87, 126; jewelry, 53; mobiles, 56
wood: balancing shapes/toys, 54, 57; boats, 135; horse, 72; houses, 70; printing, 32; pull toys, 51; rope winder, 87; stilts, 74–75

xylophone, 130

yarn. See string

Ann Sayre Wiseman is an artist, teacher, craftsperson, and mother of two grown sons. After spending several years as program director of the Boston Children's Museum visitors center, as well as conducting workshops in creative methods and materials for teachers, she had created hundreds of illustrated instruction sheets on how to make wonderful things. These recipes and ideas were compiled and became MAKING THINGS and its sequel, MAKING THINGS, BOOK 2, which were both first published in the 1970s and have been favorites of teachers and parents ever since. Revised to combine the best selections from books 1 and 2, this updated edition introduces the joy of making things to a whole new generation of fans.

Ann is also the author of: RAGS, RUGS AND WOOL PICTURES; MAKING MUSICAL THINGS; BREAD SCULPTURE: THE EDIBLE ART; CUTS OF CLOTH; RUG HOOKING AND RAG TAPESTRIES; FINGER PAINTS AND PUDDING PRINTS; WELCOME TO THE WORLD: THE BIRTH OF KITTENS; TONY'S FLOWER; DREAMS AS METAPHOR; and NIGHTMARE HELP. In addition, she produces various desk-top publications, including her many travel sketchbooks, under her own Ansayre Press. For the past fifteen years, she has been a member of the expressive therapies faculty at Lesley College, in Cambridge, Massachusetts, and now offers workshops at home and abroad. She lives in Cambridge and spends her winters painting in Mexico.

"What we learn to do, we learn by doing"
— Aristotle

HAND PRINT PRESS

QUICK ORDER FORM

PLEASE LIST THE BOOKS YOU WANT, BY TITLE & QUANTITY:

TITLE .... QUANTITY

____

____

____

____

____

____

____

SHIPPING INFORMATION

PLEASE PROVIDE ADDRESS, PHONE, AND/OR EMAIL:

____

____

____

____

PAYMENT & SHIPPING

US: $3 for the first book, $2 each additional (media mail)
CANADA: $5 for the first book, $3 each additional (air mail)
INTERNATIONAL: $10 the first book, $3 ea. addt'l (air mail)
Send check or money order, US CURRENCY only, to:
POB 576, Blodgett OR 97326
For more info: www.handprintpress.com
541-438-4300

BOOKTRADE:

Our distributor to the book trade, except for the Sundial book and Earth Art catalog, is Chelsea Green, www.cheseagreen.com, 1-800-639-4099.

HAND PRINT PRESS
QUICK CATALOG

"WHAT WE LEARN TO DO, WE LEARN BY DOING" — ARISTOTLE

***The Best of Making Things, A Handbook of Creative Discovery,* by Ann Sayre Wiseman, 178 illustrated pages, paper, budget edition, child-sized at 6x9 inches, indexed. $8.95**

125 projects carefully selected by the author to "develop natural curiosity and self-esteem," and to demonstrate "simple and important concepts that have shaped the cultures of the world." So when a child asks, "what can I do," you can say: "Make paper from laundry lint! A bird feeder from clothes hangers! Chocolate pudding finger paintings! Fish & potato prints! A cardboard box loom to weave on! Simple shirts, pants or dresses!" The author's detailed and delightful drawings fill every page: "so that children just starting out and grown-ups who have missed out can quickly grasp the ideas."

***Build Your Own Earth Oven, A Low-Cost, Wood-Fired Mud Oven, Simple Sourdough Bread, Perfect Loaves,* by Kiko Denzer, 134 pages, color photos, paper, indexed, 7x10 inches, $14.95.**

If you can make mud pies, you can make an oven. *And* bake really good bread! Simple, straightforward, inspiring, & fully illustrated "Creative. Innovative. Brilliant. ...the definitive book on how to build an adobe oven. – *www.williamrubel.com*. "Brief, brisk, artful, and well-written....empowering throughout." – *Permaculture Activist*. "...should be part of most public library collections." – *Library Journal. 5 stars on Amazon.*

***Dig Your Hands in the Dirt, A Manual for Making Art out of Earth,* by Kiko Denzer, 128 pages, 32 in color, paper, hundreds of photos and drawings, 5-1/2x8-1/2". $12.95.**

Mud is fun! Also durable, varied, easy, and dirt cheap, it has been used for millennia to make beautiful homes as well as temples and decorative art — an ideal material for the serious-but-fun work in this book: use it to make bird-houses, model villages, sculpted benches, playground structures, stunning wall murals, even monumental labyrinths and sundials! Hundreds of photos (32 color pages) feature inspiration from the US and abroad. Covers drawing and design; locating and mixing mud, sand, and other materials; architectural and philosophical perspectives; working collaboratively; and resources. An outdoor companion to *Making Things*.

"I love this book!...Every grade school teacher should seize on [it] to enrich their students' lives" — Betty Edwards, author, Drawing on the Right Side of the Brain. *"...offers a fascinating process to help you see and understand pattern in nature. The resulting designs are utterly consistent with the process of natural design. It's an invaluable and unique tool.* — Ianto Evans, author, *The Hand Sculpted House*.

***Make a Simple Sundial: Measure the Earth, Discover the Cosmos,* by Kiko Denzer, 32 pages, paper, 4-1/4x7 inches, illustrated, $4.95.**

How to make an accurate sundial with simple materials. Also walks you through a direct procedure for locating true north that will help you feel the earth turning underfoot. Gain an experiential understanding of time and the the axis it turns on. See how your dial models the relationship between the earth and the sun – and between you and the cosmos.

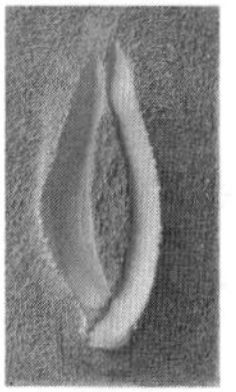

***Earth Art, A Catalog,* by Kiko Denzer, *24 pages of full color photos with text, paper,* 8-1/2 x 11 *inches,* $20.**

Unusual & beautiful natural shapes and patterns in earthen plaster.

ORDER FORM ON OTHER SIDE